Biblical Studies

Essays in Honour of William Barclay

Biblical Studies
Essays in Honour of William Barclay

edited by
Johnston R. McKay *and*
James F. Miller

COLLINS
St James's Place, London, 1976

William Collins Sons & Co. Ltd
London · Glasgow · Sydney · Auckland
Toronto · Johannesburg

ISBN 0 00 215058 1

First published 1976

Set in Monotype Baskerville
Made and printed in Great Britain by
William Collins Sons & Co. Ltd, Glasgow

Contents

The Contributors

Neil Alexander, M.A., B.D., S.T.M., is Senior Lecturer in New Testament Language and Literature in the University of Glasgow.

Hugh Anderson, M.A., B.D., PH.D., D.D., is Professor of New Testament Language, Literature and Theology in the University of Edinburgh.

R. S. Barbour, M.C., M.A., B.D., S.T.M., is Professor of New Testament Exegesis in the University of Aberdeen.

Ernest Best, M.A., B.D., PH.D., is Professor of Divinity and Biblical Criticism in the University of Glasgow.

Matthew Black, M.A., D.D., D.LITT., F.B.A., is Professor of Biblical Criticism and Principal of St Mary's College in the University of St Andrews.

George B. Caird, D.PHIL., D.D., F.B.A., is Principal of Mansfield College, Oxford.

Robert Davidson, M.A., B.D., is Professor of Old Testament Language and Literature in the University of Glasgow.

Ronald H. W. Falconer, O.B.E., M.A., B.D., D.D., was formerly Religious Broadcasting Organizer, BBC Scotland.

A. M. Hunter, M.A., B.D., PH.D., D.PHIL., D.D., was formerly Professor of New Testament Exegesis in the University of Aberdeen and Master of Christ's College.

George Johnston, M.A., B.D., PH.D., D.D., LL.D., is Professor of New Testament in McGill University.

W. D. McHardy, D.PHIL., D.D., is Regius Professor of Hebrew in the University of Oxford.

Johnston R. McKay, T.D., M.A., B.D., is Minister at Finnart Parish Church, Greenock.

William Neil, M.A., B.D., PH.D., D.D., is Warden of Hugh Stewart Hall and Reader in Biblical Studies in the University of Nottingham.

J. C. O'Neill, B.A., PH.D., is Professor of New Testament Studies in Westminster and Cheshunt Colleges, Cambridge.

Charles H. H. Scobie, M.A., B.D., S.T.M., PH.D., is Professor of Biblical Studies and Head of the Religious Studies Department, Mount Allison University, Sackville, N.B., Canada.

The Editors

Johnston R. McKay, M.A., B.A., is Minister at Bellahouston Steven Parish Church, Glasgow.

James F. Miller, M.A., B.D., is Minister at the Old Parish, Peterhead.

Editors' Preface

No one who knows William Barclay, speaks with him or listens to him can fail to be impressed, not only by his total dedication to discovering and communicating the message of the Gospel, but also by his deep awareness of the biblicality of all things and all subjects. Historical and social issues, scientific and ethical problems, current crises and future hopes, William Barclay brings all these into sharp focus under a biblical lens. This biblicality, the viewing of all things from, and the bringing of all issues to a biblical vision, characterizes the life and work of William Barclay.

The essays in this volume, written by those with whom William Barclay has worked or been associated during the course of his teaching career, cover a wide range of scholarly interests and vary in their method of presentation. Thus they faithfully reflect the breadth and diversity of William Barclay's own work. The essays have been arranged, with one exception, in a mildly canonical order. Following two personal recollections and a theological consideration of the Bible as the word of God, there are essays on matters of current interest to those working in the fields of Old Testament, Intertestamental, and New Testament studies. Professor McHardy's article has for technical reasons been placed at the end.

We are privileged to have been involved in the production of a volume intended to honour a man whose work we have admired, whose energy we have envied, and whose company we have always enjoyed.

We must express our thanks to the contributors for their help and encouragement, to Mrs Susan Mackenzie of the Chaplaincy Centre in the University of Glasgow for her work in the early planning stages of the book, to Mrs Betty McKay for her patience and skill in typing the manuscript, and to all those at Collins Publishers for their advice and understanding.

Johnston R. McKay
James F. Miller

A Personal Appreciation
Johnston R. McKay

If one of those surveys, beloved of the social scientists, were taken to find the churchman's name most familiar to the general public in Scotland, it is safe to assume that it would be William Barclay's. Yet familiarity to the public – or even popularity – is not perhaps the best criterion for judging a man's worth and his contribution to the Church. It is one of this writer's deep convictions that work in the parish is what counts most, and the contribution of a churchman outside the parish ministry is to be judged by whether it helps such work. If we apply that criterion, some cherished reputations lose at least something. Let us see what happens when we ask the question: What influence has William Barclay had on the parishes of Scotland?

The first and most obvious answer to this is the impact he has had on succeeding generations of students. He has been teaching since 1947, so that a considerable number of students have passed through his classes.

There is a tradition in the Church of Scotland that her ministers look back with awe and respect on those who taught them. Like most such traditions, it has been modified in the post-war years. It is unlikely that many of Willie Barclay's students look back on him with awe – unless it is at the amazing energy he has demonstrated. But certainly they look back with respect for his learning and personality; and with affection, for no teacher in a Divinity Faculty has made more friendships with his students.

There is, I believe, one significant distinction between the impact an older generation of teachers had on the ministry and that which Dr Barclay has exercised. The older generation of students were thoroughly taught – perhaps too well taught – so that when they found themselves in a parish, they echoed their teachers. They were imprisoned in a system of thought and it took time for them to break free. This has certainly not been the case with those who passed through William Barclay's classes. Whatever his merits as a scholar, not even his best friend would claim that he is a systematic thinker. There have been – and maybe still are – teachers who impose a system of thought on their students, who, if it is not too harsh a word, brainwash them into a way of thinking. Barclay has been too fecund a thinker to reduce his thought to a system and so we have been spared a Barclay school of thought among our ministers.

More positively, his teaching has impressed two things on his students. The importance of words and their meaning has always been driven home by him. Whatever defects Barclay has as a scholar – and he himself would admit to many – he is a superb linguist. Oddly enough he is almost unaware of his learning in this field, but many others have been unaware of it also, and so have underestimated his powers as a scholar. Secondly, he has emphasized the importance of exegesis. Time and again he has driven his students back to ask the proper meaning of the passage. And to his exegesis he has brought his deep knowledge of the background of biblical times so that his knowledge illuminates a passage. These marks of his teaching can still be found in his former students.

One other thing he has shown them – the importance of being intelligible. His students may have disagreed with him, but they never complained about being unable to understand him.

Significant as Barclay's contribution has been through his students, it is perhaps less even than his direct effect on the parishes, for here, unlike many university teachers, he has had an impact quite unique in our day. Indeed, to find a parallel in Scottish church history, we would have to go back to Henry Drummond. Why should this be? A simple answer would be that it is because of his television appearances and this is part of the answer. But even if he had never appeared on the screen, he would have been a well-known name. This was so long before he ever appeared on it. And this was due to his writing. To steal a crack from Belloc, his intellectual faults may have been as scarlet in the eyes of some, but his books were read. Many, many people have been helped by these books to a modern appreciation of the Christian faith. These books carried learning lightly; people discovered they could understand things that had been obscure and difficult. And they were helped by them. The present writer once took his son at the age of eight or nine to hear Dr Barclay preach. As he left the boy said to his father, 'You know, Daddy, that is the first sermon I have understood from beginning to end.' Later someone took this as a criticism of Barclay; if it was, it was a criticism that could have been made against the Master whom he preaches. But the present writer still remembers that sermon.

The impact of Barclay's books is international and not peculiar to the Church of Scotland. But Scotland and the parishes of Scotland have known the man at first hand. In recent years, his health has not allowed him to preach as much as he used to, but there was a time when an invitation to preach was accepted immediately if he were free. And there was no picking and choosing of so-called important charges. The generosity of these acceptances will always be remembered with gratitude.

These are personal impressions of a parish minister and they cannot be documented. They are the impressions on one minister of a man whose books helped young and old – an old woman in an Eventide Home or a young student beginning university. It is a significant achievement. It is impossible to catch in words the even greater influence of a warm, loving personality whose friendship has been shared by so many people. No one thinks of William Barclay as perfect – certainly not Willie Barclay – but he is a man who has given much intellectually and even more of his own personality. The Church of Scotland in its parishes has received much from him. His friends can laugh at his little weaknesses and failings – they can afford to, for they know how great and how many are the gifts he has shared with them. As a notable career in the classroom ends, it is a matter for the deepest gratitude that the teaching continues and the books will still appear.

Barclay the Broadcaster
Ronald Falconer

At the height of his television fame, and no doubt because of it, Professor Barclay was invited to deliver a lecture to a learned society in Helensburgh, a town on the Clyde estuary with a reputation for upper-class attitudes. This being the case, the society's secretary explained to the Professor that they were accustomed to having their lecturers appear in evening dress.

Accordingly, on the given date, Willie Barclay decked himself out in stiff-shirted finery and drove off to the burgh which claims John Logie Baird, inventor of television, as one of its sons. At that time, before his more recent illness, Dr Barclay was a heavy smoker. As he passed through Dumbarton, another Clydeside burgh, in almost every way other than Helensburgh, he realized that he was out of cigarettes. He stopped his car and hurriedly entered the first place that sold them, to find himself in a typical Scottish, working-class pub, its atmosphere blue with smoke and the language of the shipyard and football-terracing. Not unnaturally there was a sudden silence as this gleaming white apparition appeared at the bar. Then a Clydesider pointed at him: 'Hey, mister! Ah ken you! You're yon fella Barclay that does thae talks on the telly! Is that right?' Yon fella Barclay confessed that it was so. 'Weel then, Ah've a question fer you!' And at once the occupants of the bar crowded round him and erupted with question after question about his talks, about religion, about the Kirk and the common man, all tinged with that friendly aggression which is the hall-mark of the Scottish worker in his home territory.

When finally Willie Barclay was able to tear himself away from them, the men all lined up and insisted on shaking hands with him, and, as he relates in his own characteristic way, 'They paid for my cigarettes, forbye!'

This kind of scene is by no means unique. It has been re-enacted in a wide variety of places, from university common-rooms to hotel lounges all over Scotland. It is equally certain that it would happen in an even more ebullient way in the bars and common-rooms of Australia and New Zealand, were he ever to visit these countries. For there too the impact of 'The Sermon on the Mount' and 'Jesus Today' was such that the secular press ran feature articles, seeking the secrets of his television communication. The common people – and the not-so-common people – have heard him gladly. Multitudes, quite outside the Church's normal influence, have sat at the feet of one of the most remarkable communicators of New Testament teaching in this or any other age. This is an undeniable fact which the Church has not taken seriously for a number of reasons, not all of them honourable.

Professor Barclay was already an established radio broad-caster before television came north of the border in 1952. His contributions to the Light Programme 'People's Service' were regular and popular. Similarly, his 'Lift up your Hearts' early morning talks on the Scottish Home Service took a grip on all sorts and conditions of men and women, including the young student, about to commit suicide, who was arrested by something he said, sought him out, and was able to take a saner look at life as a result.

In a sense, his radio performance was remarkable. For twenty years ago, to succeed as a broadcaster one was supposed to have a properly modulated voice, be friendly and attractive in presentation, intimate and yet largely without accent. If it hadn't been for what he said, and the way in which he said it, Willie Barclay would certainly never have passed a BBC audition test. Almost everything he did, by way of technique, was wrong. To begin with, the voice was harsh; he spoke very quickly indeed, with a strong accent. There was no sense of pause, of emphasis, of short, compelling sentences. It was full steam ahead from the moment he began to speak. He quite literally broke all the known rules. In a few years' time he was to do so all over again, with television his 'victim'.

We were fairly sure that he might establish himself as a television performer as he had done in radio. But now we found a reluctant star. For years he would have nothing to do with the newer and more complicated medium. Regularly, twice a year at least, he was invited to do television; equally regularly he refused, politely but firmly. Of course, television was – and still is – an intimidating medium. 'Those ghastly cameras', said George MacLeod of Iona, 'resemble nothing so much as a four-barrelled trench-mortar pointing straight at you!' Strong, blinding lights pour in on the victim, silent cameras and cameramen move here and there, apparently aimlessly, but all under the control of a distant and unseen director. No audience, no listeners, only a highly automated, electronic atmosphere which is modern 'show business'. Into this the nervous cleric is led, patted reassuringly on the shoulder by a young imp half his age, and told, unavailingly, just to 'relax and be yourself'! Anything less like the pulpit and the lecture-room, with their captive, sympathetic, if somnolent audiences, would be difficult to find.

Willie Barclay frankly confessed he was afraid of facing the cameras.

He remained so until his good wife, Kate, told him, after the manner of good wives, that he was a coward and should have a go at it. So with the greatest reluctance, but to our immense delight, he indicated he would be willing to try a short series of programmes, provided he could have some of

B

his beloved students with him, 'to make me feel more at home', as he said. Naturally we were more than willing to go along with that. Accordingly we devised a studio format in which, after the convention of such programmes, he would expound some New Testament teaching, and then answer the students' questions. The students, incidentally, were a well-chosen group which included some brilliant academics together with mature men entering the ministry after a career in some other profession or trade.

The programmes were recorded in 1962 in BBC-Scotland's temporary studio at Springfield Road, Glasgow, this being the former 'Black Cat' cinema, within a longish stone's throw of Celtic Park. The moment we saw Willie under the cameras, all of us, production staff, cameramen, engineers, who were involved in making the programmes, became quite sure that we had before us, on the electronic screens, a unique 'winner'. My colleagues were fascinated by this extraordinary, fluent, forceful character, out of whom spilled exact knowledge, brilliant illustrations, humour, stories, entertainment, in one vast, inseparable and compulsive whole. A little later, viewers' reactions were precisely the same. As the series got under way, letters poured in, saying, 'This man is terrific! Give us more! He doesn't argue about religion [as was the custom of the then BBC "Meeting Point" programmes], he tells us in a completely understandable way.' Most of the letters then went on to say, 'But who were the young men asking all those complicated questions of the Professor? They got in the way – lose them!'

About the time that we had to make up our minds as to whether we should proceed with another series, I had a discussion with a number of intelligent parish ministers, albeit with 'high-church' leanings. Had they seen Dr Barclay's series? If so, did they think we should do a further series? While not all of them had seen the programmes, they voted about 20 to 1 against such another series! This was largely on often obscure theological grounds (and prejudices) which would leave the common man completely cold. We decided to go ahead, this time amending the series in the light of the adverse reactions.

Now we were able to plan in terms of 'Glasgow, Studio A', the newest and largest television studio outside London. We arranged to have a studio audience of some sixty people to whom Willie Barclay would speak, and, still obsessed with the 'Meeting Point' approach, the last ten minutes or so of each programme were to be given over to questions and discussion arising from the lecture. We were given an evocative set by our design people; we gathered our audience from several churches and groups with articulate laymen; we flooded them all with lights and manœuvred cameras around and about them in the best light entertainment style, and hey presto! we had a second series of Barclay programmes!

The reactions were even more lyrical than on the first occasion. Indeed, at our BBC-Scotland regular programme-review meeting, attended by producers and heads of departments, up spoke David Hanley, the Scottish film unit manager: 'This Professor Barclay that Ronnie's got on on Sundays is the most terrific character I've seen on television for many a day!' He then added, more reflectively, 'In fact if there'd been a few more ministers like him around when I was young, I mightn't be an atheist today!' But viewers were still firmly against 'audience-participation'! 'Give us Barclay by himself!' they all demanded. Now at that stage of religious broadcasting development it was heresy to propose that any man should appear alone in front of cameras, however able or brilliant he might be. Dialogue was all; how dare we thrust any opinions down people's mental throats without being open to questioning, dispute, and indeed outright confrontation on matters of fundamental belief and disbelief! All this, despite the fact that in other spheres all manner of 'experts' were given their own programme series to put over their gospels simply, so it seemed, because they made 'good television' or added up to the ways in which individual producers and series' producers looked at life. This attitude was so entrenched, even in my mind, that I tended to reject the idea that 'Barclay by himself' should be given the freedom of the screens, even upon a subject on which he was an obvious expert and popularizer. Then, just when I was near to agonizing over this dilemma, a very ordinary thing happened.

The Professor preached one morning in Newlands South parish church, where I normally worshipped when not committed to Sunday broadcasts. I had never seen and heard Willie Barclay preach before. I was totally fascinated! There he was, in a smallish pulpit, but wholly caught up in his subject. He moved around the pulpit with great vigour; he gesticulated, waved his arms, pointed his finger, turned this way and that, adjusted his hearing-aid – and all of it with complete naturalness of expression. As I watched, it dawned upon me that we had been trying to make Barclay conform to the conventions of television, both in placing him inside a specially designed studio set, and, what was more important, in submitting him to the inevitable questioning of the day – always a hazard with him because of his hardness of hearing. What we should attempt to do next was to bring the cameras and the lighting into his own, natural, speaking environment, and there try to capture him in full flight. Certainly, if he could in any way reproduce the freedom, the humour, the character of that sermon, preached in a somewhat cramping physical situation, we should have a winner!

And that was precisely what we had and did for the next six or seven years, until Willie himself said, 'We've done enough for now; we'll take a rest for a year or two.' (Even in that proposal he was unique; no other regular broadcaster in my experience ever said, 'Enough for now!')

All his programmes were worth watching. The man himself fascinated viewers. At the height of his success (for such it was), as many people were watching the Barclay lectures as watched the then 'Top of the Pops' in religion, the still-with-us 'Songs of Praise'. Yet the series which seemed to go deepest and hold most viewers were the ones upon the life and person of Jesus of Nazareth. 'A People's Life of Jesus' made a great impact, as did 'Stories Jesus Told', with 'The Sermon on the Mount' perhaps the most popular of them all. We ended his consecutive run of programmes with 'The Sermon', although two years later he was to return, at the joint request of the Baird Trust and BBC-Scotland, to deliver the last series undertaken before I retired in 1971, the Baird Lectures of 1970, on 'Jesus Today: The Christian Ethic in the Twentieth Century'.

What was the secret of his enormous success in television? My friend, the Rev. James Peter, Director of Religious Programmes for the Australian Broadcasting Commission, got as near the truth as any when he wrote, after Australia had seen 'The Sermon on the Mount' and 'Jesus Today':

I do not recall any series of programmes prompting so many letters and other expressions of appreciation. Long after we had shown the last of them I was (and am) still being told that Barclay's lectures were among the best things we have ever put on. From time to time I try to determine why these programmes made such an impression on so many different kinds of people. A priori one would have thought that such a format (a professor lecturing in a classroom) and such a piece of talent (walking up and down, clumsy of build, marked accent) would spell disaster on television. The answer lies, I feel sure, in the truth and relevance of what he had to say, along with his patent sincerity.

From across the Tasman Sea, the Rev. Michael Jackson Campbell, Director of Communications for the Presbyterian Church of New Zealand, expresses the same mixture of admiration and puzzlement:

As far as I know, William Barclay has never visited New Zealand. Yet his name is a household word here, and his form and features well-known through the length and breadth of New Zealand.

All this has happened in a comparatively short time. In fact, within the last three years. About three years ago we looked sceptically at a pilot television programme presented to us by Dr Ronald Falconer of BBC-Scotland. Of course we knew Professor Barclay from his reputation as a writer and preacher, but there is a sturdy independence about New Zealanders that requires even overseas 'greats' to come to the bar of our local judgement.

When the pilot programme finished, there were dark mutterings amongst the professionals. 'He does it all wrong.' 'He walks about like a caged lion.' ' "Talking head" programmes are strictly for hunters.' Then quite suddenly there was a short silence and some startling innovator dared the hazard, 'BUT he really got through to me!'

The programmes were played, they were an instant success, and everybody, like Oliver Twist, asked for more – and got them.

It was not that these programmes touched everyday church-goers, or sermon-tasters, or even self-appointed theologians. They touched everybody right throughout New Zealand. On Monday mornings people talked about them in trains, buses and lifts. Young executives with long-haired elegance, and mutton-freezing factory workers with an earthy turn of phrase, all debated what he had said. The programmes set ordinary people talking about important religious things, and as they talked, they found that what they were saying was really important to them.

Many people are still wondering why it all works. What the appeal of Willie Barclay really is. Perhaps it is because in a society that claims to have written off preaching, we are really hungry for it. Perhaps it is because he talks to us with human understanding and with wit and humour. Of one thing there is no doubt. He speaks to us because he really believes that what he says matters and he communicates to us that we matter; and for us ordinary folk, all this adds up to the fact that he makes his faith live and his God real. No wonder the cry goes up, 'Bring back Barclay!'

When I visited New Zealand in 1971, I showed various types of religious television programmes to mixed seminars of NZBC staff and clergy of all denominations. At the first of these, in Dunedin, the Scottish city, documentary films, discussions, and the ever-popular 'Songs of Praise', came in for that forthright criticism to which Michael Jackson Campbell referred. Last of all came Barclay in full flight in 'The Sermon on the Mount'. There certainly was absorbed silence as all watched the screen, but I steeled myself for the outburst as the programme ended. Outburst there certainly was, much more cheering than I had anticipated. Our chairman, Terry Bryan, the lively senior executive producer in charge of southern New Zealand, shot out of his seat and exclaimed, 'By God, that's the best religious television I've ever seen – even if I did disagree with many things he said!' That kind of reaction was to be repeated all over New Zealand. In Christchurch, the extrovert Anglican dean of that city demanded, 'Why can't we see this man in New Zealand?' In Wellington, the capital, an NZBC young producers' course was fascinated by the lecture and one young Kiwi summed up what he'd seen, in his own vernacular: 'She's a beaut!' In Auckland the dean's question was repeated and a combined seminar of NZBC staff and clerics made a united and vociferous demand for Barclay. At last all these pressures penetrated to the NZBC and the church planners, with the results Michael Jackson Campbell has so graphically described.

Thus New Zealand and Australia – in which latter country 'The Sermon on the Mount' was repeated three times in each state. The story of Professor Barclay's television work in the United Kingdom, outside Scotland, is less encouraging. The BBC-London religious broadcasting staff, during the sixties, were unbelievably arrogant towards the rest of Britain. I have heard the then Head of Religious Broadcasting, and his assistants, say at different times, 'Of course, the only *good* programmes are made in London!' By a 'good programme' they largely meant the kind of intellectual discussion which takes place in school and university staff common-rooms. This attitude was fostered by the BBC hierarchy of the day. 'The only people that matter for you', said one BBC television magnate to a religious department conference, 'are the people who read the *Sunday Times* and the *Observer*.' When I suggested, in discussion, that Christ died for all men, and that the common people heard him gladly, there was a furious riposte. As for Barclay, he was just another 'talking head', a preachy type of old-fashioned character who typified the out-of-date and out-of-touch television London expected from nationalistic, reactionary old Scotland. Thus, when James Peter from the Australian Broadcasting Commission saw a Barclay programme and fell for it at once, he had a complicated and difficult task persuading London to let him hire it for his ABC. Truly, in their eyes, no good thing came out of Scotland.

As the sixties drew towards an end and the seventies began, a remarkable change came over the London scene, aided by change of personnel. Helped by James Peter's demands and those of a host of English, Welsh and Irish churchmen, BBC-London agreed to put out 'The Sermon on the Mount', albeit well after 11 p.m. on Tuesday nights. Even at that late hour, the reactions were lyrical from all over the country. For me, however, the richest moment came at a United Kingdom conference of religious broadcasting staff. There I heard a senior London man rave about 'The Sermon' in such ecstatic terms as to suggest that *he* had discovered this fabulous communicator and that the Great British Public must have more of him! It was useless to point out that the Great Scottish Public had already had him for eight consecutive years; that each and all of these programmes had been offered to London, and rejected by London for a variety of reasons, both theological and tele-visual.

London was accordingly offered the next series, 'Jesus Today: the Christian Ethic in the Twentieth Century'. After viewing this series, they took cold feet and rejected it on the grounds that Barclay was not really 'with it' in terms of the contemporary attitudes to sexual morality (or lack of it), and that ethics were, strictly speaking, not his line of country either. Yet the fact remains that every word Willie Barclay uttered in these his Baird Lectures was firmly based, in terms of his own deep, New Testament understanding. His preparation for these lectures was to read the whole of the New Testament afresh and most of the Old Testament too, in order to come to a *scriptural* understanding of the Christian ethic, not only in the personal and sexual field but in the industrial and the international areas as well.

This London rejection was typical of their paternalistic attitudes for at least three-quarters of my twenty-six BBC years. With great soul-searching, and sometimes agonizing, they came to a belief about what was really best for listeners and viewers. This was chiefly a projection of their own likes, dislikes and confusions. Programmes and people who did not add up to their peculiar insights, especially Scottish programmes, were just not seen south of the border. Yet some of these liberal men would fight the idea of censorship to the death! But such was their own blindness that they did not recognize another form of it in their own policies. Perhaps these explanations will make sense to the large numbers of English, Welsh and Irish churchmen who have asked me, over the years, the Dean of Christchurch's question, 'Why do we not see Willie Barclay in this country?'

All regular religious broadcasters must face the burden of pastoral caring. People who would not dream of going near either a church or a minister or priest frequently write to broadcasters who impress them, often pouring out the most complex and harrowing stories. Willie Barclay drew more than his share of such correspondents. Many of those who watched him were impressed by his common touch and deep humanity. They took to him instinctively. Here was a man to whom they could tell their troubles; who would understand their human condition. Thus his 'fan-mail' was much more than a collection of 'thank-you' letters. This was brought home to me vividly when I rang him about 9 a.m. one morning to discuss an urgent point in his next broadcast. The engaged signal. I told my secretary to keep on ringing until we got him; this she did at regular intervals, with the same result, until just before midday. By this time I was more than a little frustrated. 'Willie, you've been on that phone all morning!' 'Well, it's your fault!' 'What on earth do you mean by that?' 'When I'm doing a television series, I have to spend two mornings a week, and two evenings as well, phoning folk with pastoral problems, as well as both writing and seeing them.' That answer humbled me, I must confess. All this – added to his university lectures, his writing of many books and his speaking and preaching engagements.

Once, at the end of a successful series, he and I were reviewing reactions, of which there had been many, especially asking for more. I told him that most of the letters we had received in the BBC had come from people in trouble, 'the lame, the halt and the blind'. I suddenly realized that his eyes were brimming over. After a long pause, he said, quite simply, 'It makes you feel right humble to be used in this way.'

What, then, is the real secret of the success of this most fascinating communicator of New Testament teaching, through the modern medium of television? There are several strands to it, and some have been indicated already. First of all, his preparations were meticulous. We discussed the content of a series as early as six months before it was seen. All that time the programmes were germinating in his mind and spirit. His scripts were largely memorized, although every word was written down. Not only so, but, however weary, he always insisted on a complete run-through of each broadcast before the cameras, in the empty lecture-hall. He was slow to come to television, but having arrived, he treated it with the utmost respect of the true professional. In all television, even the most casual, there is no substitute for homework.

Next, he was brimful with his subject. He was so much in love with it that his joy and happiness in what he was saying flooded over, infectiously, to his vast, fireside audience. In addition, his subject-matter was directly and simply expressed, although he had no hesitation in turning to the blackboard and writing up the Greek and even the Hebrew for his key words. No talking down here. All of this was brilliantly illuminated by stories taken straight from everyday life. He had, indeed, studied closely the teaching method of his Master, Jesus of Nazareth, hence his parables from everyday life.

Then he had the immense advantage of being a genuine 'character', the sort of personality who at once attracts attention, with his harsh voice, his vivacious manner, despite his considerable bulk, his gestures, even his ever-present and often whining hearing-aid. Up and down his rostrum he pounded, stopping to emphasize a point, then off again with a whirl of his arms. His total being, physical, academic, spiritual, was caught up into one unforgettable whole of dynamic communication. He ranks with the great 'natural experts' of television communication – the Mortimer Wheelers, the Arthur Neguses, the Patrick Moores and the Brian Horrockses.

But for me his ultimate secret, which is no secret at all, is his profound personal devotion to the Jesus he seeks to show to people. The Christ is explained, magnified, commended, and ultimately glorified by one who loves him very deeply.

The Bible — Word of God?

R. S. Barbour

No man of the present generation in the English-speaking world has done more to bring the Bible to the people than Professor William Barclay. Through him indeed 'the Bible speaks again'.[1] Yet he would probably be among the first to agree that neither the interpretation nor the status of the Bible is an easy topic for us to handle today; and while the study of the Bible (and of his own commentaries and books about it) expands into ever new territory in other continents, in the Western world there is a 'strange silence of the Bible in the Church'[2] and a widespread assumption outside the Church that the Bible no longer has any relevance for contemporary questions. Missionaries returning to Britain within the last few years, coming fresh to the situation, have been deeply struck by the rapid decline in the position of Christian education and biblical knowledge in the schools, and it is only too obvious that, whatever they may think of the Bible, most young people are not enthusiastic adherents of the Churches. What has gone wrong? In this situation, and by way of a tiny tribute to a great biblical expositor, it is perhaps fitting to survey one or two aspects of the scene in which we find ourselves with regard to the Bible.

What has gone wrong? The man who writes from the conservative evangelical point of view has his answer: We can no longer hear the Bible as the word of God. Why? Because of the uncertainties caused by biblical criticism, which has shaken our hold on the truth. 'From the start, biblical criticism drove a wedge between revelation (the Word of God) and the Bible (man's written witness to the Word of God). It viewed the Bible as a library of human documents, fallible and often fallacious, and defended this as the only "scientific" view.'[3] Our only hope is once more 'to identify the writings with the Word'.[4] It is not my purpose in this short essay to enter into dispute with that position. I must confine myself to saying that it is simply not possible today honestly to identify the writings with the word, if by so doing we are committed to the view that the scriptures do not err either on matters historical or on any others. Biblical criticism has done something that can never be undone; it has forced us to take the Bible seriously as a library of human documents, whatever else it may be, and from the theological point of view not to take fright but to rejoice in the liberation which that has given us. It *may* be true that some of us can no longer hear the Bible as the word of God; it must be true that we *ought* no longer to hear it as the word of God in the way in which many of our forefathers heard it. But that is not to say that we ought not to hear it as the word of God at all. A good deal of recent discussion about the Bible has departed from the use of the phrase 'word of God', and this is reasonable enough; there are other ways of viewing the significance of the Bible. The contention of this essay is simply that we should not lose sight of the phrase altogether.

The concept of the word of God, like that of inspiration, originates for the Christian with the Old Testament picture of a God who speaks, using the prophets to declare his will in human words. God speaks, through the prophet, in the first person: 'I am He, I am the first, and I am the last' (Isa. 48:12). The long process by which the phrase 'word of God', which originally referred to God's utterances, came to be applied to written material, much of which contains no utterances of God at all, need not detain us. But most Christians have to some extent retained the ancient Hebrew way of understanding God and his utterances, and given that starting-point, it is not surprising that God should be held to speak to men through or by means of the scriptures, as also in preaching from the scriptures; and in Christ himself, who stands at their culminating point and whom the prologue to St John's Gospel describes as the Word. This threefold sense of the 'word' – the word written, the word preached, the word incarnate – has been used in this century, notably by Karl Barth, as the foundation for our understanding of the Bible and indeed of theology as a whole.[5]

Since it is no longer possible to think of the whole Bible as 'word of God' in which God speaks directly, inerrantly and infallibly to man, that threefold sense of the term 'word' offers at first sight a promising alternative. Theologically speaking, the primacy belongs to Christ, the Living Word, and to him the written and the preached word bear witness. The Bible, then, is essentially witness to Christ, and to the God who is God and Father of our Lord Jesus Christ. It is human, historical witness; not itself revelation, but witness to God's revelation. If we ask 'Is it trustworthy witness?' the answer must be given along two lines: (1) historical: the Bible must prove itself at the tribunal of historical criticism as a reliable witness; and (2) theological: here the answer may take different forms, but it is in any case likely to include a reference to the Spirit of God, either as having inspired or guided the biblical authors (difficult as that is to state convincingly today), or as giving us the assurance, when our hearts burn within us, that this is indeed God's truth; or both.

Here further questions immediately arise. With regard to historical reliability: if the Bible were simply to be regarded as witness to what God has *said* in the narrow sense, historical enquiry could hardly get under way. Either God has said something or he has not; either he speaks or he does not, and the historian as such cannot answer these theological questions. But of course what God has said must be interpreted in wider terms; it includes what he has done (word and deed are no doubt very closely related in the Bible), and most notably what he has done as well as spoken in the sending of Christ — his life, death and resurrection. Here events are being reported, over a period of more than a millennium, and historical criticism can and must be brought to bear. If the events did not occur as they are reported, the witness of the Bible seems likely to be to that extent discredited. But events (and words) only become significant when they are interpreted and placed within an explanatory context, and at this point history and theology become inextricably intertwined. It is at least possible that an event might be quite incorrectly reported and yet thereby be interpreted in a way vital for the understanding of God's relations with his people; the report of the escape from Egypt in Exodus 12–15 is an obvious candidate for examination in this respect.

We should also notice that whether an event be adequately or erroneously reported, if thereby genuine light appears to be thrown on God's relations with his people, it will not do simply to say that the Bible is human witness to God's revelation to man or to his dealings with man. Even if we leave aside the difficulties which many have encountered in coping with the concept of revelation itself, we have to notice that the revelation comes not through the word or act of God only, but through the response to it also; indeed, if the very reporting of the deed or act is held to be part of the response, it comes through the response only; and it is hard to see how it could come in any other way. And, as we have seen, in some cases it comes not through a reported word or deed as faithfully interpreted according to the canons of historical criticism but through the very human interpretation which, from an historical viewpoint, is distorted or exaggerated. It is not only the word or deed believed to come from God but the believing response to that word or deed that generates the revelation, and at first sight there seems to be no necessary correlation between historical accuracy and theological fruitfulness in the interpretation of the words or deeds concerned.

This leads to two considerations which must be kept before us. First, the Bible specifically in its revelatory capacity is not only 'word of God to man' but 'word of man to man' and of course 'word of man to God'. At this point the analogy between the two natures of Christ and the divine-human nature of scripture, which was much canvassed at one stage of recent debate, does seem to be relevant. Christ himself can also be said to be all these things. But the analogy is precisely not an argument from the two natures of Christ to the dual nature of the Bible as consisting of 'divine words', which are inspired and infallible, and human words, which are not. The human word, the human response (or even lack of response), which from an historical point of view may be sadly inadequate as an account of events, is or can be incorporated into the very word of God itself. The divine word is there in the human words, fallible as they certainly may be in some cases, and not anywhere else. It does not follow that the Church, which has always striven to maintain the sinlessness of Jesus in his human nature and has often also striven to maintain the inerrancy of the scriptures, ought now simultaneously to abandon both these convictions. Like all analogies, this one breaks down; and quite possibly breaks down at the point just indicated. Enough has been said at least to show how difficult the 'divine-human' analogy is to manage when it is applied to any doctrine of scripture.

The second consideration arising out of the foregoing is that the biblical account of historical events, alleged or real, everyday or miraculous, may in fact have wandered so far from any account acceptable to secular historians that it becomes impossible to relate the two accounts satisfactorily. It has often been observed, in criticism of theories which understand the Bible as essentially a record of God's mighty acts or a 'history of salvation', that the relationship between this *Heilsgeschichte* and world history or secular history is extremely hard to state. We have to face the possibility that the two may be incapable of being related to one another without contradiction, at certain stages of historical enquiry, or that the concept of *Heilsgeschichte* may lose almost all contact with 'secular-historical reality'. But perhaps we should not be too sceptical about the possibility of constructing a viable doctrine of salvation-history: the difficulty may prove eventually to be less great than existentialists and others have made out.[6] In any case, this question can only be decided by actual historical and exegetical work; the point here is that the possibility of such a breakdown must be faced. Wherever genuinely historical work is involved this kind of risk must be taken. It is of the very essence of our modern possibilities for understanding the Bible, both from an historical and from a theological point of view, that it be not protected *a priori* from any honest criticism, however mistaken; if the truth is there, it will survive. (See 1 Esdras 4: 34–41, which is in the Roman Catholic Bible, if not (yet) in the Protestant.) Many theologies can be criticized on that score, not only from the 'right wing', Catholic or Protestant, but from the 'left': for example the kerygmatic theology of Rudolf Bultmann, which seeks to disengage a gospel message that is not subject to the changes and chances of historical research into the origins of Christianity.

We are to understand the word of God, then, as disclosure of God's words and deeds — of his *will* — first made to and through his people long ago and renewed in every generation since then, by a process the nature of which is a subject on its own. We cannot say that the Bible is that word of God, but we can say that it mediates it or that it becomes it as the *viva vox evangelii* sounds in our ears. And all depends on certain 'saving events' or 'words of God' which occurred in the past but reverberate or re-echo increasingly in the present and into the future.

But further difficulties crowd in upon us, and we must allude briefly to some of them.

(1) There is much in the Bible that is neither 'words of God' (in the sense in which the Old Testament prophets, and presumably Jesus,[7] spoke 'words of God' that can become 'word of God') nor 'acts of God' (as, for example, the preservation of Joseph's life, the Exodus, the Babylonian exile or – a different kind of act here – the Resurrection may be said to be acts of God). How are we to explain the presence of material so diverse as the books of Esther, Job, Ecclesiastes and Proverbs, the Psalms, the New Testament *Haustafeln* or the Epistles of James and Jude? Can all this materail mediate or become 'word of God' today? Presumably so: we continue, in theory at least, to preach from it and read it in church. But if so, our definition of 'word of God' will have to be modified. Nor must we forget that we have no advance guarantees that the oracles of the prophets in the Old Testament, written down almost entirely by anonymous scribes, or the words of Jesus in the New, represent exactly the words actually spoken; in certain cases we may be quite sure that they do not: nevertheless they can and do become 'word of God', and our theory must provide for that.

(2) The concept of an act of God raises great theological and philosophical difficulties. But real as these are, I am convinced that without some such concept no specifically Christian theology can be constructed, and this is in any case a question that cannot be tackled here. Something similar perhaps needs to be said about 'word of God' – an idea that is often mysterious to adherents of other religions. We cannot finally dispense with it.

(3) The kind of approach to the Bible which has been outlined seems to demand a restriction of words and acts of God to the limited periods of history covered by the biblical books, a restriction which becomes more and more offensive to more and more people in our simultaneously expanding universe but contracting planet. Where does the history of

salvation begin? At creation? With Abraham? What was happening during the intertestamental period? And what has been happening ever since apostolic times? These too are questions which cannot be dealt with here. If answers can be given, it seems likely that they will lead us away from the simple stress on a history of salvation which has been so characteristic of the last generation of biblical scholarship, especially in Britain.

(4) The last question in the previous paragraph leads to another urgent topic which has dominated much recent discussion of hermeneutics. The Bible comes from a world very different from ours. It is argued that we can no longer make its prescriptions normative for today, as our forefathers attempted, with very varying success, to do in the past. Indeed, the formation of a canon of authoritative 'holy scripture' regarded as binding has even been seen as a mistake.[8] Here we introduce a whole series of further questions, many of them concerned with the way in which the Church actually has used and does use the Bible, many of them concerned with ethics, each of which must be tackled separately. The only point which can be made here is that the discerning of analogies and continuities between biblical and contemporary situations must never be avoided, as if the situations were somehow mysteriously the same; but the discerning of analogies never constitutes the whole process. I give one example. 'Reformation teaching discerned a very strong analogy between Judaism, or Judaizing Christianity, on the one hand and late medieval Roman Catholicism on the other; and this insight lies at the roots of Protestantism.'[9] The analogy is now almost worn away; but it 'continues to work in the mind of every evangelical clergyman who discerns in his people a struggle between a trust in "good works" and a "saving faith". There are, of course, differences: his parishioners, for instance, are not in the slightest inclined to have themselves circumcised or to keep the Mosaic law; but he pushes these differences aside as irrel-

evant. By contrast, a thoroughgoing cultural relativism would rate the differences so high as to leave no significant similarity at all.'[10] The author just quoted sees behind this difference the question: 'Is there then a constant reality which we call "human nature", or is it so culturally diversified that no constant elements remain?'[11] And there is indeed this question; but there is also the question: Does the Bible itself throw any light on this last question? If it does, can we accept it, and if it does not, what criteria can we use to settle the issue? There is no end to these questions, and they cannot be avoided. Whether we speak of demythologizing, remythologizing, existential interpretation, or, at a slightly different level, of the guidance of churchly tradition and 'the products of the Spirit in the Church',[12] we are seeking to find the right means of transition from the biblical world to our own and also (and perhaps better) from our own to the biblical. In this we always need, but can never easily assume, some consensus about how to go about our task. In this tension *ecclesia militans* must live. There is no advance guarantee or formula for the relation of biblical material to 'word of God' in this area; people are continually looking for it but it is not to be had. This brief reference to the problem of the authority of the Bible leads to:

(5) The question of biblical theology or theologies. James Barr has stated his belief that 'in the whole movement for the revival of biblical authority, this was what was really sought; *that the theology or theologies of the Bible should be normative for all subsequent theology*'.[13] Such a function of the Bible could be comprehended within our understanding of the phrase 'the word of God', but, as he points out, the statement just made is not a conclusion which can be drawn from the premise that the Bible records the saving acts and words of God. The theology or theologies of the Bible draw on many facts or factors and have come about as the result of many influences, some of them from outside the life and

culture of Israel and the Church. In that respect they are no different from the theologies of today. And to say that the Bible is witness to certain words or acts of God is not the same thing as to say that the theology or theologies it contains should be normative for subsequent theology. If that proposition is to be accepted as portraying a desirable state of affairs the concept of the word of God must be expanded to make this possible.

A necessary preliminary to, or part of, that theological task would be a more adequate characterization of the Bible at the historical-critical level (always bearing in mind that to distinguish this from the theological level is to make a somewhat artificial abstraction). Barr's own formulation runs: 'The status of the Bible is something implied in the structure of Christian (and Jewish) faith',[14] and he speaks of 'its status as the classic model for the understanding of God';[15] in this are included both the knowledge and understanding of God achieved in Israel and the faith in Christ of the New Testament.

As a description of the actual state of affairs a formulation of this kind is more satisfactory than many. (1) In so far as theology is always an explication of the fact and implications of faith, it would seem to be consistent with the statement that the theology or theologies of the Bible should be normative for all subsequent theology – just *how* they should be normative is a further question. (2) It points at least to the way in which the books of the Old and New Testaments alike actually came into constant use – 'not by a conscious or authoritative discrimination, but by the instinct of believing men for the relevant'.[16] But what a formulation of this kind does not do is express the conviction, which is a matter of faith, that the Bible is the *irreplaceable* model for the understanding of God and of faith in Christ; that the classical model is also the final model. A classical model might be replaced by another, which would then become classical. On the other hand, to speak of a model (an 'in' word anyway just now) does allow a necessary openness with regard to the relation of the model to that which is modelled upon it; and as we move further in time and in other respects from the world which the Bible portrays, this openness is of increasing importance.

A further feature of models is that they carry no necessary reference to history or historical events, and this may draw our attention to other features of the Bible which we cannot ignore. The Bible provides certain great paradigms, archetypes, images and myths by means of which man's place in the world can be interpreted and illuminated; on which the imagination of Western man at least has largely fed. Some of these myths or images have been historicized as part of the interpretative process;[17] others are political or social in origin, and have moved beyond their original scope;[18] 'word of God' can certainly be found here, in a sense which is to be identified neither with the actual words of the Bible nor with such words and deeds of God as may be reported in the telling of the material. Indeed, all kinds of material from within the Bible (it is usually assumed) can become 'word of God' when they are read in the light of the whole biblical context.[19] The word of God, then, is to be further characterized as God's continuing controversy and relationship with all men in all aspects of their life, as revealed to and accepted by them and as set forth once and for all in the pages of the Bible.

But that brings us up sharp against two more large questions: that of the proper methods of biblical interpretation, and that of the canon of scripture. Only two comments can be made here.

(1) The biblical interpreter's traditional resort, in passages which he cannot interpret literally to his satisfaction, has been to allegory; and beyond that, in certain cases, to other 'senses of scripture' (e.g. the moral and anagogical senses of ancient hermeneutical theory). But alongside those approaches and others like them which are in essence attempts to do justice to the whole of the Bible as one solid body of

sacra scriptura, there has always been the tendency to evaluate some parts of the Bible more highly than others, whether or not this leads in effect to the formation of a 'canon within the canon'. Historical and critical honesty compel us today to admit that this will always and inevitably happen, without denying that the existence of the canon is a warning against its dangers. But on any tenable view of inspiration and of apostolicity (here I must simply state my conviction dogmatically), the canon itself does not constitute a hard-and-fast frontier outside the limits of which no writings can be found which will mediate the word of God to his people today, in the same way as it is mediated by the scriptural books themselves.

(2) But if that is so, we are brought up against one final difficulty which attaches itself to any modern attempt to reassert the status of the Bible as 'word of God'. Put bluntly: Does God no longer speak to his people as he did through and to the Old Testament prophets, through (and to?) Jesus of Nazareth, through and to the earliest Christians? Are 'those former ways of God's revealing his will unto his people . . . now ceased'?[20] The scriptural reference attached to the phrase from the *Westminster Confession* just quoted is Hebrews 1:1; and indeed, the only basis on which the statement could be accepted is that God has spoken *finally* ('in this the final age', NEB) in the Son. But that in turn poses sharply the question of the eschatological proclamation of the New Testament, so pervasive throughout its pages, so much discussed and canvassed 'in these last days' of this century, which are nevertheless not the last, but only the latest, in a process of history of unknown duration. It may be true as a general proposition that the delay of the parousia did not profoundly affect the structure of early Christian belief and theology (as against the theses of Martin Werner and others). It is also true that to live permanently in the expectation of this glorious hope under the mythical

forms in which it is expressed in the Bible is not easy. But if it can be done it must be done in the realization that the thrust, both of the Bible itself and of the tradition which has always accompanied it and of which it is part, is or should be towards the completion of God's purposes in the future. God *does* speak to his people as – but always *as* – he spoke through the prophets and in the Son; it may be one of the services of the modern Pentecostalist movement to and in the Churches that it compels us to see this, even if only in a limited area.[21]

It is time to draw this survey of problems and questions to a close. The Bible is indeed to be heard as the word of God still today, both as the record of God's decisive saving words and deeds which continue in his relationship with his people, and as – in some sense not here defined – the norm for all theological reflection and indeed also for all the other needs of the Church. But the Bible is not 'word of God' in its own right as something perfect, inspired or even dictated by God and standing, as it were, independently of the Church, which receives it, uses it, and stands under the authority of the word, which is that of God himself.[22] In his book *The Foolishness of God*[23] J. A. Baker has written: 'If it could ever be proved that the Gospels consisted of completely accurate material for a biography of Jesus, the traditional Christian faith would collapse in ruins . . . Every one of the systematic edifices of belief, both orthodox and heretical, which have marked the history of Christianity has depended in the last analysis on an edited, expanded, or artificially interpreted version of the gospel text.' Some might retort that those statements reflect not the foolishness of God but the foolishness of J. A. Baker. Yet the point he makes with regard to the Gospels, even if overstated, is substantially true for the Bible as a whole. As received, interpreted, understood and evaluated by the Church and by critical scholarship, but also as listened to obediently, both by the scholar with his reverence for the text and by those who know that life has sprung forth from its pages and will do so again, the Bible can become — and indeed in a decisive sense *be* — 'word of God' for any man anywhere. Günther Bornkamm, in an eloquent address, has shown this with regard to certain passages in the Gospels and the Pauline Epistles.[24] But is the same true, at least in principle, of all the varied material of the Bible, much of which can only be read as remote oriental legislation, as awful warnings of the folly of human cruelty, as primitive superstition, and so forth? In so far as it is all part of *our* history — the history of a people confronted by a mysterious, but a just and merciful, God whose purpose thrusts forward towards the summing-up of all things in Christ — the Bible's very variety, its richness of reflection of the multifarious human situation, its genius as literature, endow it with the capacity of becoming 'word of God' today. And why not so with any other literature? I see no reason why not — sometimes; but only against the background of the Bible. And why is that? Because, in the end, Israel's God is not like any other God: in Christ he was made man, and the simplest human word can become one with God's word, cutting through our evasions and hesitations, restoring us in the very moment in which it has exposed us. But this is the work of the Spirit and the Word, and is beyond the historian's ken, as it is beyond that of the literary critic — unless it breaks through to them precisely in the exercise of their craft. What the historian and the literary critic can see, however, and have alas all too often seen, is what can happen when the Bible ceases to be understood as God's humble human instrument in their hands and becomes — as the Church also can become — a thing which possesses its own perfection and a weapon in the hands of men. As Edwin Muir put it,

> The Word made flesh is here made word again
> And God three angry letters in a book,
> And there the logical hook,

On which the Mystery is impaled and bent,
Into an ideological instrument.

Perhaps it is right that a poet should have the last word. For poetry too can be truth, and can become God's word to us; and the Bible is full of poetry, a fact the deep significance of which has been far too little appreciated 'in these last days'. The Bible has suffered much from having its poetry turned into systematic theology; although there too the word of God can sometimes be heard.

The Old Testament —
A Question of Theological Relevance
Robert Davidson

In 1901 there appeared a book by the then Professor of Old
Testament Language and Literature at Trinity College,
Glasgow, George Adam Smith, entitled *Modern Criticism and
the Preaching of the Old Testament*. Its basic presupposition was
thus succinctly stated: 'Modern criticism has won its war
against the traditional theories' (i.e. about the Bible). 'It
only remains to fix the amount of the indemnity.'[1] The
author was unduly optimistic. At least some sharp skirmish-
ing remained. The book provoked protest in the United
Free Church Assembly and was the subject of a committee
report. George Adam Smith was defended in the Assembly
by, among others, his Glasgow colleague, Professor James
Orr, who, while dissenting sharply from some of the ration-
alistic speculations in the book, warmly defended the
Christian devotion, evangelical zeal and scholarly integrity
of the author. No ecclesiastical action was taken against
George Adam Smith. The theological climate of opinion had
changed since the day – but twenty years previously – when
William Robertson Smith had been stripped of his teaching
post in the United Free Church College in Aberdeen for
advocating precisely such modern historical and literary
criticism. After his dismissal William Robertson Smith
carried the battle to his ecclesiastical opponents through a
series of public lectures, published as *The Old Testament in the
Jewish Church* (1881) and *The Prophets of Israel* (1882). In the

preface to *The Old Testament in the Jewish Church* it is claimed: 'The great value of historical criticism is that it makes the Old Testament more real to us . . . In all true religion the new rests upon the old. No one, then, to whom Christianity is a reality can safely acquiesce in an unreal conception of the Old Testament history; and in an age when all are interested in historical research, no apologetic can prevent thoughtful minds from drifting away from the faith if the historical study of the Old Covenant is condemned by the Church and left in the hands of unbelievers.'[2] It was part of the greatness of George Adam Smith that he took the tools of criticism and showed how they could help the Old Testament to be a living reality for faith in his generation.

The war was over, so it was claimed; nor was the indemnity daunting. *Modern Criticism and the Preaching of the Old Testament* sought to demonstrate how modern criticism had helped to separate the wheat from the chaff. The pure revelational strand in the Old Testament now stood out clearly – its unique development of ethical monotheism, a development which culminated in the great prophets of Israel.[3] The prophets were indeed the liberal Protestants of ancient Israel, evangelical in fervour, anti-sacerdotal in practice if not in principle, servants of a sensitive social conscience. For the rest, in both the Wisdom literature and in the narrative sections of the Old Testament there was much that was 'immortal with truthfulness to the realities of human nature and of God's education of mankind',[4] much to appeal to the enlightened ethical insight, many anticipations of Christ's teaching.

I have begun with George Adam Smith because we can see clearly today how, brilliant expositor and Old Testament scholar that he was, he was still very much the child of his age, and his insights – particularly the emphasis upon ethical monotheism and the prophets – were the partial insights open to his age. This is said, not to condemn George Adam Smith, but to remind ourselves that we are in precisely the same boat. We dare not claim finality for our theological evaluation of the Old Testament; it will reflect the concerns, the questions, the problems and the intellectual presuppositions of our day and age. One thing, however, has become clear. The indemnity was to prove far greater than George Adam Smith envisaged. There has been a widespread failure of nerve in our *theological* handling of the text of the Old Testament. For many there is a tacit assumption that the modern critical approach to the Old Testament is theologically insignificant or irrelevant, if not destructive. In the pulpit and in the life of the Christian community there is evidence for what has been well described as 'the strange silence of the Bible in the Church';[5] in the case of the Old Testament the silence has, at times, been deafening.

Let me give you a pulpit example. The text was taken from the Joseph narrative, from that poignant moment when news was brought to the aged Jacob that the son whom he had long considered dead was alive and eminently successful: 'But when they told him [Jacob] all the words of Joseph, which he had said to them, and when he saw the wagons which Joseph had sent to carry him, the spirit of their father Jacob revived' (Gen. 45:27). In particular, the words 'when he saw the wagons' were emphasized. It was a sermon preached not long after the Women's Voluntary Service had begun a 'meals on wheels' service to the shut-ins in the community – 'when he saw the wagons' . . . It was an excellent sermon on community responsibility and caring, but it is hard to see why it had inflicted upon it these unsuspecting words from Genesis. A concordance consulted in desperation late one Saturday night seems the most likely explanation of the link between text and sermon. It is tempting but hardly reasonable or wise to blame the preacher in this situation. One of the most widely used Bible commentary series, 'The Interpreter's Bible', is an open invitation to play this schizophrenic homiletic game. In the format of the series the critical commentary is done by one scholar, an academic; the homiletic, sermonic, devotional material by another, hopefully a preacher-scholar. The relationship between the two is, to put it mildly, somewhat ambiguous. Thus 2 Kings 2: 23–4: 'He [i.e. Elisha] went up from there to Bethel; and while he was going up on the way, some small boys came out of the city and jeered at him, saying, "Go up, you baldhead! Go up, you baldhead!" And he turned around, and when he saw them, he cursed them in the name of the Lord. And two she-bears came out of the woods and tore forty-two of the boys.'

The critical exegesis by N. Snaith sees this as 'merely an example of pre-moral exhortation to respect the prophets as the holy men of God. The story compares most unfavourably with NT teaching . . . and indeed will not stand examination from any moral point of view.'⁶ The homiletic section by R. Calkins then takes over: 'Here is a story from which the Bible reader shrinks. A careful reading of the text, however, will show us that Elisha did not himself summon the bears. He was not that kind of man.' Then, energized by allegory, it takes off on a flight of powerful pulpit oratory: 'The bears that came out of the woods are the symbol of the inevitable retribution which overtakes vicious behaviour. The boys of the story are the prototype of thousands of youth today . . . Lawless youth may not be torn asunder by bears, but they are rent by passions, devoured by appetite, until their character and career and all their hopes for happy useful living are destroyed.'

Note what has happened. The critical exegesis has placed certain question-marks against any easy theologizing, or even moralizing, of the incident; the homiletic section has totally ignored the question-marks. It is not my concern to apportion responsibility for this situation. The critical exegesis may or may not be adequate. But, granted the fact of the divorce between the two approaches, it is the critical approach which will seem to be theologically irrelevant, and which indeed has been regarded as irrelevant in this instance.

This exegesis-homiletic impasse is curious, since, when we view the broader theological scene, there is little doubt that the Old Testament has played a significant role in the contemporary debate. Critical work on the basic structure of Old Testament theology, whether in terms, for example, of covenant relationship, *Heilsgeschichte*, promise-fulfilment, communion with God, provided much of the impetus for the growth of biblical theology, a movement which in spite of its defects, and in spite of obituary notices, is still with us and likely to remain so for some time. The work of the Pannenberg circle and the *Theology of Hope* of J. Moltmann[7] draw extensively on insights from Old Testament theology, particularly from the work of Gerhard von Rad. The exponents of a secular theology[8] have often found the Old Testament a more congenial ally than the New. Even those who wish most radically to reinterpret the Christian faith in non-theistic terms feel under some kind of obligation to justify their stance by appealing to the Old Testament. Thus Alistair Kee in *The Way of Transcendence*[9] provides us with what he admits to be a 'rough-and-ready' interpretation of the Old Testament, but one which, he claims with a certain lack of modesty, gives 'a better account of the history of Old Testament religion than the theistic interpretation given by the Jews themselves'.[10] He adds: 'A section like this has become almost obligatory in any work on contemporary theology.'[11] Theologians of the most varied persuasions seem to be haunted by the necessity of justifying their positions with reference to the Old Testament. The necessity seems to be the greater the further they move from classical theology. Sometimes one can only wonder why they don't leave the Old Testament alone; just as not a few sermons could be improved by the omission of a superfluous Old Testament text.

Inevitably certain sections of the Old Testament tend to be evoked to contribute to the understanding of our contemporary dilemmas. Just as the prophet Jeremiah was well on the way to becoming the patron saint of theological draft-card burners in the USA in the 1960s, so now the Old Testament doctrine of creation, and in particular Genesis 1, is being thrust into the centre of the theological discussion of the ecological crisis. Two recent articles are pointers in this direction: 'Creation and Environment' by John Macquarrie,[12] and 'Man and Nature – The Ecological Controversy and the Old Testament' by James Barr.[13] Although written independently, they have a considerable amount of common ground. Both are concerned with the claim which has been made that the biblical doctrine of creation, of which Genesis 1 is the *locus classicus*, is the necessary basis of the modern scientific outlook. The factors on which this claim is usually grounded are:

(1) The essential separation between God and the world in Genesis 1 – a de-divinization of nature, yet, with it, a refusal to see nature as in any sense anti-God. Science could not 'have arisen in a world where nature was regarded either as partaking in the divine or as partaking in evil'.[14]

(2) The emphasis upon man's dominion over the rest of creation in Genesis 1, which provides a philosophical *sine qua non* for a technological society. 'Technology can thus be thought of as a sort of secular fulfilment of a basic outlook about humanity which is already expressed in Genesis.'[15]

Both Macquarrie and Barr note that such a claim is double-edged. It may be used positively to affirm the significance of the Judaeo-Christian tradition as providing the essential ideological precondition for the development of modern science and technology. But there is the other side of the coin. Does this not mean – as has been increasingly urged in recent years – that biblical tradition as mediated through the Christian tradition bears responsibility for our present ecological crisis? 'By destroying pagan animism, Christianity made it possible to exploit nature in a mood of indifference to the feelings of nature.'[16]

Both are concerned to deny any necessary causal or

genetic relationship between the biblical doctrine of creation and modern science. Macquarrie, for example, points to the fact that, 'the Hebrews themselves held to a doctrine of creation for several centuries, but they developed no science worth mentioning and technically they were inferior to their neighbours in the arts both of peace and war'.[17] Barr regards it as 'enormously improbable' that the Genesis tradition influenced the rise of science or had any causal relationship to it. He points out that it is not customary for historians of science, even those sympathetic to the Christian faith, to make this claim or to regard it as in any sense significant. Moreover, the key concept of man in Genesis 1, man made 'in the image of God', has not been traditionally understood to refer to man's dominion over nature, but to man's spiritual nature, his immortal soul. Nor is man the exploiter a legitimate exegetical inference from Genesis 1. Dominion over nature is 'a fact in the text, but it has come to be over-emphasized in the kind of exegesis which made it identical with the image of God in man'.[18] What we are given in Genesis is a paradisal picture, a beginning time corresponding to the end time postulated in prophetic sources, a time of total harmony and peace in nature and in the relationship between man and the natural world, an idyllic scene presided over by man. Having denied any causal link between the biblical creation story and modern science, Barr affirms: '. . . the great modern exploitation of nature has taken place under the reign of a liberal humanism in which man no longer conceives of himself as being under a creator, and in which therefore his place of dominance in the universe and his right to dispose of nature for his own ends, is, unlike the situation in the Bible, unlimited.'[19]

What relevance, then, does the biblical creation tradition have for our contemporary problems? Barr suggests four points:

(1) There is the insistence of the Genesis story that all that was created was created 'good', surely 'a powerful motive for

all sorts of action to control and limit the exploitation and pollution of it'.[20]

(2) The world of Genesis 1 is an ordered world. Although this is a different kind of order from the scientific principle of order, there is something in common between the two which enables the theologian in the Judaeo-Christian tradition to 'view with a sense of community the researches of science, the achievements of technological control, and the work of the accompanying social sciences'.[21]

(3) Genesis affirms that man is man when he is in his place in nature; that place being less one of exploitation than of leadership, a sort of primary liturgical place. Therefore it is entirely consonant with the tendency of the Old Testament, 'that man's dominion or eminence should from now on be increasingly applied to the task of conserving and caring for the natural resources of God's world'.[22]

(4) When the Old Testament does evince a proto-scientific interest, it is located not in the context of creation, but in the Wisdom literature, for example Job 28, in that part of the Old Testament which most evinces 'an international and even inter-religious culture'. The Old Testament writers do not feel constrained to justify this interest 'by deriving it from their own religious tradition or to magnify their own religious tradition by representing it as the source of this insight. Is not this something of a good example for the Judaeo-Christian idea of creation as it associates itself with the world of science in our time?'[23] That is to say, we ought to be on our guard against any false theological imperialism.

I have concentrated on Barr's arguments because they present us with an instructive example of an Old Testament scholar seeking to deny certain inferences which have been loosely drawn from Old Testament material, but at the same time concerned to ask what may legitimately be drawn from that material in the light of our contemporary problems. This inevitably leads him to direct our attention primarily to those aspects of Genesis 1 which seem likely to be of immediate relevance. But may it not be that we can purchase this kind of relevance at too high a price, the price of ignoring the central thrust of the biblical material with which we are dealing? We are faced more radically today with a problem which has been with the Church across the centuries, the need to transform biblical concepts, images and ideas into the thought patterns of our own vastly different cultural presuppositions. How in the process of transformation do we safeguard the essence of the original? May not the cry of relevance distort or lead to the neglect of essential elements in the original? Is Genesis 1 *primarily* concerned with the goodness and order in the world, or with a doctrine of God? Is it *primarily* concerned with man in his place in nature, or with man in his place *vis-à-vis* his Creator? We must, indeed, be on our guard against using a passage in the interests of a false theological imperialism, but it is equally dangerous to use a theological document – and Genesis 1 is nothing if not theological – and neglect its original theological orientation.

What is the theological orientation of Genesis 1? Let us approach it by way of a detour. 1 Kings 18 describes the conflict on Mount Carmel between Elijah and the prophets of Baal. There may be much debatable in the tradition, but central to it is Elijah's challenge to the community to choose between two different religious allegiances: 'How long will you sit on the fence? If [Yahweh] is God, follow him; but if Baal, then follow him' (1 Kgs 18:21, NEB). After a dramatic vindication of the power of Yahweh, the community makes its decision, 'Yahweh is God, Yahweh is God.' This is the moment of triumph for Elijah, champion of the Yahwistic tradition in Israel. But it has solved no problems. It has not provided any effective answer to what was to be the continuing and long-term attractiveness of the cult of Baal for the Hebrew people. Over a century later the prophet Hosea gives voice to Yahweh's bitter complaint that Israel

'does not know that it was I who gave her
corn, new wine, and oil.
I who lavished upon her silver and gold
which they spent on the Baal' (Hos. 2:8, NEB).

It was precisely this provision of corn, new wine and oil that
the cult of Baal offered its devotees, a religion which was a
form of naturalism, the divine identified with the world of
nature in its differing aspects, and man invited through
varied rites to participate in and to forward this life, thus
guaranteeing the stability of the world-order and the continuing rhythm of the seasons. The challenge to Yahwistic
tradition in Israel – and the only effective answer to the continuing appeal of Baalism – was to develop a doctrine of
creation which would relate God meaningfully to the world
and the world meaningfully to God without succumbing to
the dangers of naturalism. This is what we find in Genesis 1,
priestly teaching propounding a doctrine of creation which is
a deliberate counter-statement to the naturalism inherent in
the worship of Baal. The indispensable nerve-centre of this
counter-statement is a radical doctrine of *transcendence*, which
refuses to identify God with the world or to divinize anything in the world, which insists that God is a reality independent of the world, the source of its life but not identifiable
with that life. 'In the beginning God created . . .' 'God said
. . . and so it was.' 'God made . . .'

It is arguable that this emphasis on transcendence is the
most meaningful contribution that the Judaeo-Christian
can make to the ecological crisis. It is questionable whether
faith has anything to contribute to that crisis, anything
distinctive, unless it can enable men to face it in the light of a
reality and hope which transcend the crisis. Certainly I do
not think we are entitled to use Genesis 1 theologically unless we allow this doctrine of transcendence to shape our
thinking as it profoundly shaped Israel's thinking. Nor is
this merely escapism. For the opposite side of the coin is that

the world and man find their rationale, significance and meaning only in relationship to this transcendent God.

The paradox which arises from faith in this transcendent God is creatively evident in the witness of the Old Testament prophets. The prophet always confronts his people with a word which comes from a God who is independent of man, his culture, his social organization and even, or should we say *particularly*, his religion. The experience of Israel suggests that religion is often the greatest threat to transcendence; thus Israel repeatedly sought the security of the naturalism offered by the worship of Baal; thus Israel too easily identified God with a holy city or a holy temple; thus Israel too readily imprisoned God within formulations of faith which proved inadequate to interpret the rich reality of life. In the light of *this* God, the prophets find themselves *totally committed* to the society of their day and *totally detached* from it. Their total commitment finds expression in their inexorable social passion – whose source is the known character of God – in their demand for social righteousness, for a reformation of society, in their searing criticism of a religion which effectively blunted the social sensitivity of men. Their total detachment finds expression in the word of judgement which envisages the breakdown of the very society for whose restructuring they plead and in the word of hope which summons men to live and to find new life in and through the destruction of everything they value in their culture and religion. In terms of our contemporary ecological crisis, total commitment, however theologically and empirically necessary, can never in itself be theologically adequate. When the scientist is speaking of doomsday and the possible breakdown of life on the planet earth, we must have a theology of doomsday which will enable totally committed men to say, 'As in the beginning, so in the end – God.' It is difficult to see how we can say this, short of some doctrine of transcendence such as lies at the heart of the doctrine of creation in Genesis 1. To put it in other terms, '. . . the sacred must always be not only ambiguous but unlimited: it is a mystery, so that no specific significance can exhaust it – there is always more waiting to be explored.'[24] But there has always been the temptation, not least in theology, to sacrifice the uncertainty of that 'more' for the security of the 'less' we think we can define and control.

The language of transcendence is today highly suspect in certain theological circles. Some of the classical models of transcendence certainly need to be modified. From an Old Testament point of view two comments may be made:

(1) The biblical models of transcendence are not always as naïve as is sometimes suggested. It is wrong to suppose that the biblical models necessarily have built into them the idea of God 'up there' or 'out there'.[25] Genesis 1, the *locus classicus* of the doctrine of transcendence in the Old Testament, uses no such models. It employs instead the verb 'create' (Heb. *bara'*), which is used exclusively of God's activity in the Old Testament, and talks in terms of the effective word, 'God said . . . and so it was.' Nor does the Old Testament use other models uncritically. The monarchical model, 'the Lord is king', found particularly in the Psalms (e.g. Pss 93:1; 95:3; 97:1),[26] is a good example. The Hebrews were only too painfully aware that the concept of kingship was ambiguous. They knew kings who used power ruthlessly and irresponsibly. Before dispensing with the monarchical model, we need to explore what precisely the Old Testament writers meant when they used this model of transcendence; what content was uppermost in their mind when they used 'king' as a description of God; how indeed the anthropomorphic model is modified by the recognition of that which the prophet Hosea puts into words, 'for I am God and not a man; the Holy One in your midst' (Hos. 11: 9, NEB).

(2) In his book *The Way of Transcendence*, Alistair Kee, in his pursuit of a valid secular faith in Christ, offers us an interpretation of the Old Testament minus Yahweh, just as he

offers us a Jesus stripped of all the God-talk nonsense. Israel may have thought of her experience as Yahweh-centred, but without loss we can relate it in other terms. 'In their terminology it involved Election and Covenant, but in its simplest terms it involved living one life and not another. It was not the obvious life to live. It certainly distinguished them from their neighbours.'[27] The way they chose he calls 'transcendent', the way of their neighbours 'immanent'. It would be idle to deny that it is possible to rewrite the Old Testament in such terms. After analysing religious experiences, Kee correctly notes that 'no experience is *necessarily* interpreted in a religious manner. It may be justified, and perhaps even correct in some sense, to give a religious interpretation to various experiences, but it is always possible for others to say that such an interpretation is inappropriate. In particular, the man who has no prior belief in God may well realize that an experience interpreted as religious by one person does not bear the weight of such an interpretation for him.'[28] True, or there could be no atheists or agnostics, nor would there be any decision element in faith. But the converse may equally well be urged: 'No experience is *necessarily* interpreted in a non-religious manner . . .' What is strange is that having opted for such an interpretation and having retained the word 'transcendent' to describe Israel's choice of what can only be termed 'not the obvious way to live', Kee is in the end driven to confess that 'at the present moment we are not in a position to formulate a satisfactory ontology which would take account of this fact'.[29]

At least the Old Testament had such an ontology, 'In the beginning God.' Short of some such ontology, it is difficult to see why we should insist on retaining the language of transcendence at all. Some modern reinterpretations of transcendence seem closer to Baalism than to the faith of Israel, as that is presented to us in Genesis 1.

A Future for Apocalyptic?

Hugh Anderson

It is a great privilege to be invited to contribute an essay in honour of a friend whom one has long held in the highest esteem and affection. The breadth of his scholarship, his remarkable powers of communication and, perhaps most importantly, the warmth of his humanity have impressed untold numbers of people. I am pleased to offer a brief study, not technical but broadly based, on a subject in which I was interested and on which I was working as long ago as the late 1940s when I first knew Professor Barclay as a senior colleague in Trinity College, Glasgow.

The word 'apocalypse' represents the Greek *apokalupsis*, which means an 'uncovering', 'unveiling', normally of something which has hitherto been hidden and is now revealed, and which occurs in this sense in Galatians 1:12 (cf. 2:2), for example. But the derivative term 'apocalyptic' is a technical one and the root meaning of *apokalupsis* does not help us very much to define its range or scope with precision, not any more than the root meaning of Gnosticism (gnosis=knowledge) helps us to define the phenomenon so described. In fact 'apocalyptic' is one of those words so variously understood by those who use it that meaningful discussion on the subject is often almost impossible. Accordingly it has lately been suggested that a term like 'apocalyptic' (and indeed the related term 'eschatology'), which may mean everything or next to nothing, depending on the user, were better dropped from our vocabulary altogether. But problems are not removed or resolved by declaring a moratorium, even if that were possible, on the use of words traditionally connected with them. We must therefore continue to make do with the designation 'apocalyptic', in the hope that the configuration of ideas it stands for may be clarified a little as we proceed.

We have to begin from the rather questionable assumption that it refers to a particular type of literature (the 'apocalyptic literature' so-called) produced in considerable volume in Jewish and early Christian circles between 200 BC and AD 100, the classic examples being the Book of Daniel and the Book of Revelation. But it should be noted at the outset that since not by any means all of the books designated 'apocalyptic' have a uniform literary structure (compare the Book of Daniel with Jubilees or the Book of Revelation with the Testaments of the Twelve Patriarchs), the term 'apocalyptic' may perhaps be more appropriately taken to denote not a specific literary *genre* but a particular *religious posture* characterized by a peculiar preoccupation with the End-time or the Last Days of the world.

Now in the Church's first age the validity of the apocalyptic standpoint was seriously questioned. Official recognition was granted very grudgingly to those 'black sheep' of the canonical family of documents, Daniel and the Book of Revelation. The latter was involved in a long struggle for canonization. From the time of Dionysius of Alexandria (around AD 260), its integrity in the East was violently shaken. Only after Athanasius in his Thirty-ninth Easter Epistle, and the Latin Church under the influence of Augustine around the close of the fourth century AD, accepted it in their canonical lists did it receive widespread sanction as a part of the New Testament. Official hesitancy in the Church about such works as Revelation is not hard to understand – their awesome and detailed portraiture of the terrible tribulations preceding the End-time and of the end of the world itself seems alien to the normative New Testament concentration on the death and resurrection of Jesus

Christ as God's saving act for all mankind. Centuries after Revelation had found its way into the canon of scripture, the Reformers still regarded it very negatively, Luther in particular, with his focus on justification by faith alone in the redemptive efficacy of Christ's death, declaring that it was 'neither apostolic nor prophetic'.

Through a very long period, then, the pall of suspicion lay heavily over apocalyptic in the Great Church at the more official level. But on the other hand the apocalyptic fantasy, with its dream of the impending overthrow of this world, had a profound impact not only on art and literature but on popular attitudes and perspectives. In his remarkable book, *The Pursuit of the Millennium*,[1] N. Cohn has shown how the peasant revolts of the Middle Ages were often inspired by the expectation that evil (manifested especially in the imperialist pretensions of ruling powers) had had its day and the old-world order was about to be dissolved and give way to a new order, which could be precipitated by active revolution on the part of the poor and dispossessed. In medieval art pictures of Armageddon and its terrors abounded, and symbolic representations of the terrible fate of the damned in fiery torment or of the ultimate bliss of the righteous gripped medieval men with horror or filled them with tremendous hope. In literature, works as diverse in type and form as Sir Thomas More's *Utopia*, Dante's *Inferno* and Milton's *Paradise Lost* owed much each in their own way to the imagery and outlook of apocalyptic. If the Great Church on the other hand for so long entertained the strongest reserve towards apocalyptic, it was possibly because, in its increasing secularization and alignment with the reigning establishment, it regarded the apocalyptic mood as a source of agitation and a spur to the fanatical fringe, or as the property of the eccentric.

In modern times certainly, albeit for different reasons, apocalyptic has also for the most part been under a cloud. Following upon the rise of rationalism and the Enlightenment, the liberal theologians devoted themselves ardently to scientific reconstruction of the genuine historical 'essence' of Christianity. In their attempts to probe behind the dogmatic crust with which they felt the authentic mission and message of Jesus had been overlaid in the New Testament, they were convinced that the apocalyptic elements were a temporary ancient integument that had to be stripped away to get at the real Jesus. Harnack's *Das Wesen des Christentums* (*The Essence of Christianity*) may fairly be said to be the high-watermark of liberalism, and it depicts an entirely non-apocalyptic Jesus, who is no visionary of the End-time but simply the supreme teacher of an ethic of the fatherhood of God and the brotherhood of man. Aside from being by-passed or excised altogether among scholarly circles in the nineteenth century, apocalyptic tended more and more to become in any case a monopoly of sectarian groups alienated from the mainstream of the Church's life, like Jehovah's Witnesses, whose doorstep visitations and recitations of the events of the End (now drawing close) are still familiar to us. More recently (1941) R. Bultmann administered what might have been thought to be the *coup de grâce* to the relevance of apocalyptic expectation for our time: 'The mythical eschatology [of apocalyptic] is untenable for the simple reason that the parousia of Christ never took place as the New Testament expected. History did not come to an end and, as every schoolboy knows, it will continue to run its course.'

Apparently, however, apocalyptic still possesses unexpected residual powers of survival, both on the academic and popular fronts. In his fascinating monograph on the subject, Klaus Koch feels able to speak in fact about an apocalyptic renaissance in the last decade or two. The factors operative in what is undoubtedly a revival (in both professional and lay quarters) may be generally described as follows:

(1) Intensive study of the Dead Sea Scrolls ever since their

discovery has built up for us the picture of a monastic sect of Judaism in the time of Jesus which not only treasured apocalyptic works but was fired with apocalyptic zeal and expectation. The covenanters of Qumran thought of themselves as the final elect of God, chosen to purify the faith of their fathers through the trials of the Last Days and engaged to that purpose in the eschatological warfare of the children of light with the children of darkness. Faced with the known existence of a priestly *apocalyptic* sect roughly contemporaneous with Jesus and the early Church, we have been forced not only to revise previous estimates of the nature of late Judaism but to ask whether apocalypticism like that at Qumran (and not just the Judaism of the Pharisaic rabbis, with its focus on the Law) may not have exerted a considerable influence on the New Testament.

(2) In Bultmann's theology of existence the stress has lain undoubtedly on the *individual*'s inward decision in encounter with the kerygma of the Cross, and on the individualizing of eschatology, whereby the *eschaton* is construed not as something God will accomplish in and with the world but as the moment slumbering *within* each one of us which only needs to be awakened. The Bultmannian individualism has lately seemed unsatisfactory to some theologians, who see in apocalyptic, with its external, cosmic dimensions, a means of broadening the horizons to embrace the larger and indispensable concern with the justification of God's cause over his *whole world*. So E. Käsemann has declared that 'apocalyptic was the mother of all Christian theology – since we cannot really class the preaching of Jesus as theology'. This has been taken up by W. Pannenberg, for instance, into a systematic treatment of the nature of history as understandable only in the light of a final situation, an ultimate goal which can be described, as in the typical apocalyptic interpretation, as the end and consummation of history. Similarly J. Moltmann has made apocalyptic, in its universal outreach beyond the question of the individual's destiny to that

of the *world*'s destiny in the *End*, the servant of a revolutionary Christian ideology.

(3) But also, in a quite different way, at the popular level, apocalyptic has been coming to the forefront. In America particularly, the apocalyptic mood has lately been given a new expression in large numbers of young people, dissatisfied with and defecting from the major denominations of the Church and institutional religion generally, creating self-contained communities of 'enthusiasts' (shades of Qumran!). It is significant that Daniel and Revelation are among their favourite biblical books. They confidently expect, many of them, that God is about to break in to destroy the existing world-order – they have after all been brought up under the steady threat of a nuclear holocaust! Whether their expectation of an imminent end to world history arises from a deep-seated pessimism about the contemporary state of things or from a revolutionary desire to see all things changed is not easy to say. At any rate the apocalyptic outlook is rife among them. In colleges and universities the present writer has repeatedly been confronted with the question: 'Do you believe in the *rapture*?' The first impish instinct has been to reply with a counter-question: 'Do you mean the first fine careless rapture or the last mad fond embrace?' But of course one knows they are asking whether one hopes to be caught up any moment now, to meet with the Lord in the clouds of the air,[2] and asking it seriously and literally.

It is against this wide background of renewed interest that we here ask about a future for apocalyptic.

Appraisal of the value and relevance of apocalyptic today is inevitably woven up with the question of what it *was* and what it *meant* among its leading exponents in the ancient period of its heyday. And here more than usually, one suspects, subjective factors influence historical judgements. A positive evaluation of the message of apocalyptic such as we find in H. H. Rowley's little book *The Relevance of Apoca-*

lyptic[3] is probably conditioned to some degree at least by the felt need at all costs to argue the abiding relevance of what appears in the Bible; a negative evaluation by the conviction that the apocalyptic posture is essentially a fringe phenomenon, peculiar to sectarian enthusiasts. As Koch puts it, 'Anyone who finds a futurist eschatology impossible today does not want to find one in the New Testament either.'

Consequently, ridding ourselves so far as possible of presuppositions about the contemporary worth of apocalyptic, we must first enquire what was the movement of mind behind the literature of 200 BC to AD 100 commonly called 'apocalyptic', leading examples of which are Daniel and Revelation within the canon, and 1 Enoch, 4 Ezra, Baruch, Jubilees and the Testaments of the Twelve Patriarchs outside the canon. It may be claimed that the term 'apocalyptic' should be reserved for a context of life and thought in which some configuration of the following features or ideas appears (whatever the literary form and structure of the work in which they are set down in writing):

(1) Ecstatic seeing or hearing appears to figure prominently. In Revelation, for example, the visionary element is stressed immediately – the seer of Patmos says: 'I was in the Spirit on the Lord's day, and I heard behind me a loud voice like a trumpet saying: "Write what you see in a book and send it to the seven churches" ' (Rev. 1:10–11). The book thereafter consists largely of a great series of *visions*. In the Book of Enoch, Enoch is transported on a great heavenly journey in which he is given a glimpse of the abode of the departed with its various compartments. To what extent the visions or ecstatic hearings reported were actual, objective experiences, like the mystical visions of the saints of the devotional life or the hearing of voices of a Joan of Arc, it is not easy to say. It is certainly difficult to imagine that the highly pictorial descriptions of the Son of man in Daniel, 1 Enoch, 4 Ezra and Revelation (e.g. Rev. 1:12–19), couched as they are in Old Testament language, were any-

thing more than a stylized literary form. Even so, though the vision-report is merely a stylistic device, its very frequency attests the crucial significance of the visionary element for the readers to whom these works were first addressed.

(2) The apocalyptic visionary operates with a large and powerful lens, so to speak, and is able to discern the measurable epochs into which God had predetermined that all history should be divided from the time of creation itself. Above all, he depicts, in bizarre and often grotesque imagery, the vast cosmic catastrophe that is about to befall in the near future.

(3) The cosmic canvas on which the apocalyptic visionary paints his pictures is heavily peopled with angels and demons, locked in the final conflict of good and evil in the Last Days. Wanting from the pure Yahwism of the classical Hebrew prophets, the angelology and demonology that were to be extensively developed in the late apocalyptic writings are widely held to have been imported into Jewish religious thought from oriental sources in Zoroastrianism.

(4) Beyond the coming cataclysm the seer detects a new divine order resulting from God's ultimate victory over evil and consisting of a return at the End of the paradisal beginnings (the myth of the restoration of the lost original paradise being pervasive also in primitive tribal religions, as Mircea Eliade and others have shown).

(5) For the seer, God's victory will mean the winding up of earth's proud empires for ever and their replacement by God's rule.[4]

(6) Sometimes the apocalyptic vision alludes to a special divine emissary who will help God to execute his purpose in the consummation of history (e.g. 'one like a son of man').

How influential for Jesus on the one hand or for early Christianity on the other was this constellation of ideas? The brief treatment of the question on which we must venture here is scarcely proportionate to its importance for determining the historical decisiveness of apocalyptic. At the close of his monumental *Quest of the Historical Jesus*,[5] written early this century, Albert Schweitzer portrayed Jesus as ablaze with thorough-going apocalyptic zeal and grasped by the absolute conviction that God was about to break in to foreclose world history even within his own lifetime: then, when his hope was not realized and the End did not take place, he surrendered himself to a martyr's death on the cross in order to hasten its coming. But in relation to the whole gospel tradition the portrait, it may fairly be claimed, is reductionist or one-sided. Over against the Jesus who seems to predict the coming heavenly triumph of the Son of man (see, e.g., Mark 14:62) or the imminent advent of the kingdom of God (Mark 9:1), we have to reckon with numerous other aspects of the gospel witness to him. We have to reckon with the Jesus of the parables – the parables of the kingdom particularly indulge in no speculation about the End-time, but challenge the hearer to the faith that can recognize the tokens of the *hidden presence* of the kingdom of God in, with and around Jesus in his ministry. We have to reckon with the wisdom factor in Jesus' teaching, the notion of the continuous providential care of God over his whole creation (e.g. in the Sermon on the Mount, Matt. 6:25–34). We have to reckon with his categorical repudiation of all such cosmic signs or portents as were part of the stock-in-trade of apocalyptic: 'Why does this generation seek a sign? Truly, I say to you, no sign shall be given to this generation' (Mark 8:12). All in all Jesus does not appear as the one who uniquely 'fleshed out' the typical apocalyptic expectation. Rather he shares with the Hebrew prophets that 'shortening of historical perspective' which discovers in the realities underlying the present situation the certainty that the time appointed by God is drawing near. So he renews and transforms the present moment for men by calling them towards a future in which this *one* thing will be true: God will reign! And that is a far cry from the apocalyptist's massive concentration on calculation of epochs, seasons, dates and events leading up to the End.

The case with the Apostle Paul is rather different. That he did participate in a Jewish apocalyptic heritage is clear enough, even if we look only at 1 Thessalonians 4 and 1 Corinthians 15. His use of apocalyptic symbols and terminology is not in doubt. Nevertheless, that his earlier apocalyptic hopes, revealed in 1 Thessalonians, were subsequently greatly toned down and reorientated towards the *individual* and his destiny by the time of 2 Corinthians (see chapter 5) is still a distinct possibility that must be entertained. It is of course true that the visionary element was a feature of Paul's life, witness the accounts of his conversion experience in Acts and his own highly condensed reference in Galatians (1:15–16) and the Acts report of his vision of the 'man of Macedonia' (16:9–10). But to hold that Paul lived his Christian life in the grip of the overmastering apocalyptic idea that he was God's last emissary delegated through Christ to precipitate the end of history by missionizing the Gentiles[6] is to go much too far. While Paul's life and thought are directed towards the consummation God would bring in the (near) future, apocalyptic expectation is surely not the whole of Paul. The apocalyptic 'tendency' in the apostle is in fact clearly refined by the specifically Christian understanding of existence, for which the 'new creation' or the 'new man' *has already* become a reality through the redemptive death of Christ.

Are there then any indications of the impact of the apocalyptic posture on early Christianity aside from Jesus and Paul? E. Käsemann has argued that such indications do in fact exist, that the oldest presentation or interpretation of the Christian gospel resides in a post-Easter apocalyptic. According to Käsemann the Easter experience opened the gateway to an apocalyptic interpretation of the kerygma that took the following lines:

(1) a history of salvation and a history of damnation run-

ning parallel to each other and broken up into separate epochs;

(2) a transmutation of values and the twelve tribes of Israel re-established in the Last Days;

(3) confirmation of the Law of Moses and antipathy to the Gentile mission;

(4) hope of the epiphany of the Son of man in his parousia. Possibly, if pressed for a short definition of apocalyptic, Käsemann would say that it is that peculiar style of interrogation which combines the question of God with the question of the future of history, of which the coming glory of the expected Son of man is the main sign in the early Christian milieu.

But it is very much open to doubt whether late Jewish apocalyptic was so homogenous a phenomenon as is here supposed – we have to take greater account not only of the salient differences between the books labelled 'apocalyptic', but of the remarkable diversity of symbols and ideas entering the pseudepigraphical literature, probably from a matrix in Hellenistic-oriental syncretism. Even more seriously, there is little if any evidence in the New Testament to support the contention that post-Easter apocalyptic was the earliest expression of the Christian gospel. Indeed the evidence seems to point the other way. In what is possibly the most primitive kerygmatic formula we possess in the New Testament (1 Cor. 15:3ff.) there is no mention of the Son of man or his parousia. Again, in early Christianity, the hope of what God *will* do never swallows up the saving assurance of what God *has already* done in the life, teaching, death and resurrection of Jesus Christ. The conviction in the first Church that God *has* disclosed himself in the world in Jesus leads to a Christian 'worldliness' and away from apocalyptic 'otherworldliness', and so overcomes the pessimism characteristic of the apocalyptic mood. Not scribal mathematics or geography of the End and the events accompanying it, but the missionary proclamation of the 'good news' of what God *has* accomplished (the sole ground of hope) is the overriding concern in the Church's earliest age.[7]

Perhaps the most crucial consideration of all is this: If late Jewish apocalyptic were so formative and determinative for the first formulations of the Christian message, how is it that there is nothing remotely comparable in the New Testament to the Book of Revelation until about the close of the first century AD? Such apocalyptic segments as exist before that are relatively few and peripheral (e.g. 1 Cor. 15:20ff.; parts of the Thessalonian correspondence; Eph. 3:3f.; Heb. 12:22–9). The so-called 'Little Apocalypse' of Mark 13 is in the last analysis actually *anti*-apocalyptic: Mark here uses apocalyptic materials (many of them scarcely authentic words of Jesus) as a cover for *paraenesis* or exhortation to the Church of his day, and the exalted Jesus who speaks here really offers correctives to apocalyptic fanaticism (see, e.g., Mark 13:32f.: 'Of that day or that hour no one knows, not even the angels in heaven, nor the Son, but only the Father. Take heed, watch; for you do not know when the time will come').

If, therefore, the characteristic literary form in early Christianity is the Gospel (narrating God's act in Jesus), and to a lesser extent the missionary or pastoral letter, bearing witness to a life that *has been lived* and a way that *has been travelled* for the salvation of all mankind, what are we to make of the Book of Revelation with its involvement in speculation about the hoped-for future? Now, to be sure, Revelation is variously evaluated. On the negative side, it has been characterized as a 'weakly Christianized Judaism' where the present is a time of temporariness and no more, or a little less negatively, as a *Gelegenheitsschrift*, a valuable monument from a single crisis in the history of Christian faith (the time of the Domitianic persecution) and no more. On the positive side, it has been maintained that the message of Revelation is indeed genuinely and fully Christian in character and abidingly relevant – the God who revealed himself in Jesus is on the throne despite turmoil on earth and his final victory is sure.[8] Whereas, on this view, it must be conceded that the Seer aims to show that his own period is the period immediately before the End, nevertheless he does look to that End in hope as the future in which the Church will live with Christ who appears in glory and who, as the lamb that was slain, bestowed the forgiveness of sins on the cross; so believers in the Church are confronted here and now with the past, present and future Christ. However, it should be noted that within this general framework there remain a-Christian or sub-Christian relics, the cry for vengeance in 6:10, for instance, that suggests the Apocalypse is in danger of 'falsifying God's goal with the world'.[9] Arguably, therefore, for all the Seer's grasp of what God has achieved in Christ, it does not altogether save him from making a leap from the 'now' of contemporary history to a disjunctive 'then', so that his visionary pictures of the geography and history of the End-time become a kind of palimpsest obscuring the lineaments of God's saving work for man in the present moment of his existence.

Our admission is accordingly that Revelation hardly overcomes the weaknesses inherent in the typically apocalyptic posture. The intention of the author is seemingly not to promulgate a theology of history, but to promote the certain imminent expectation of the existing world's overthrow. The imminentist eschatology of apocalyptic appears to go hand in hand with a 'world-weariness', a historical pessimism, a 'loss of world' that arises from the surety that the cosmos must be completely overthrown by a divine cataclysm before renewal can take place. In this connection the thesis bears scrutiny that the Gnostics' world-dread of late antiquity is a legacy from Jewish-Christian apocalyptic.[10] Is the rapture – expectation of some contemporary young people which we remarked on earlier – a replication of this world-dread in late Western culture? It may be just that, more an escape from the effeteness of a civilization that has apparently run down than an expression of revolutionary optimism! Further, it may be claimed that the strange and often quite cryptic symbolic language that is the medium of communication in apocalyptic is especially liable to materialist or literalist interpretation, so that instead of fostering a rationally respectable philosophy of history, it simply engenders an irrational preoccupation with mapping out calendars of the fast-approaching End. This is nowhere more in evidence than in the recurring crudely fundamentalist understandings of Daniel and Revelation, particularly among 'adventist' sects. More seriously still, the exclusivism or narrow electionism of apocalyptic groups, the unshakeable belief that the small circle of the chosen alone will be saved on God's coming Day of Judgement while all evil 'outsiders' will be condemned, this constitutes a grave hazard to the fullness of the Christian gospel, contrasting radically as it does with Jesus' own open invitation to *all needy sinners*. In the book referred to above, N. Cohn speaks of the collective megalomania of apocalyptic communities and traces a link between that and the revolutionary chiliasm of the Middle Ages, as well as a link between apocalyptic fantasy and modern totalitarianism.

Yet, however negative one's estimate, there is, it must be conceded, a future of sorts for the apocalyptic world-view, possibly, for many, an *unwanted* future. In advanced contemporary societies the majority of men no longer look for a god or gods to irrupt into history suddenly and dramatically to wrap it all up for ever. They organize methodically and proceed scientifically in attempts to programme the future. But even now, amid all the tensions of the time, men do still sometimes resort to millennial wish-dreams. As Bryan Wilson observes in the conclusion of his encyclopedic work on *Magic and the Millennium*:[11] 'In day-dreams, fantasy and dreams men accept magical solutions to personal and perhaps social problems . . . The search for the unprogrammed in the increasingly programmed society is a commentary on the persistence of the demand for fantasy. The demand for fantasy reminds us of the untamed, perhaps untameable element of man's spirit.'

But to leave the matter there, as though apocalyptic were no more than the product of man's demand for fantasy, would be unjust. There is in fact a dimension of the apocalyptic outlook that is proving fruitful in current reformulations of Christian theology. Ever since the Enlightenment the trend has been for Christian theology to be isolated from cosmology (or from nature) by the natural sciences, and to be rarefied into anthropology (as most recently with Bultmann). The referent of theological thought has thus become man's spirituality, subjectivity, personality or selfhood. The works of Käsemann, Moltmann and Pannenberg can be seen as attempts to overcome this 'inwardizing' or individualizing of theology. They seek to revive apocalyptic as providing symbols that constrain the imagination to go beyond the frontiers of the individual life and reckon with the cosmos – God's purpose is not just the salvation of the individual but the justification of his cause over all the created order. But while one would not wish to undervalue recent efforts to re-pristinate the apocalyptic posture as a means of arousing a historical, future-directed faith, one should not be blind either to the lively dangers inherent in apocalypticism in its ancient, as in most forms of its modern, expression. Moltmann to his credit has noticed this quite clearly: 'Apocalyptic was frequently speculative and narrated the events of the last times as if they were past history. But only the past can be narrated; the future has to be historically anticipated in word and deed . . . The Christian certainty of hope becomes practical in the transformation of the present.'[12]

Whether apocalyptic in its classical form (the same would apply to modern manifestations) awakened a social consciousness that struggled for the transformation of the present, or whether it did not rather encourage sufferers in the present evil age merely to endure the worst in the passive expectation of a better hereafter soon to be inaugurated, this is the burning question that requires a more elaborate treatment beyond the scope of the present paper.

Eschatology and Politics:
Some Misconceptions

George B. Caird

Not long ago I heard of a college library where it was discovered that a book on primates had been catalogued under 'Ecclesiastical History'. From my own experience of the workings of the academic mind it would not have surprised me if some scholars had come forward to defend that classification. For some years past I have been protesting against a similar aberration in the library science of biblical literature. I believe that those writings which we have been taught are apocalyptic, which are rightly held to be one of the principal formative influences on New Testament thought, ought not to be catalogued as 'Science Fiction' (of the Doomwatch variety), but as the 'Theology of Politics'.

Ever since Johannes Weiss and Albert Schweitzer set eschatology at the centre of New Testament teaching, it has proved an embarrassment to those who retain an interest in the credibility of the Gospel. Either Jesus expected an imminent End, and he was wrong; or the early Church so thoroughly misunderstood him as to attribute to him this erroneous belief. It is hardly too much to say that eschatology has been the greatest single obstacle to the quest of the historical Jesus. Because of eschatology Schweitzer himself ended with a Jesus 'who comes to us as One unknown, without a name',[1] speaking to us out of a discredited world-view. Because of eschatology Bultmann found himself forced (though far from unwilling) to demythologize the

New Testament and leave us only with existentialism. Even Dodd, who spoke more sense than most on this subject, granted that the early Church had misunderstood Jesus and recast his teaching in the mould of Jewish apocalyptic. Kümmel, rejecting Dodd's solution in favour of the belief that Jesus himself was mistaken, grappled with the theological implications of this, only to emerge with a solution of his own indistinguishable from Dodd's. More recently Conzelmann has argued that Luke totally transformed the primitive tradition he received, substituting for eschatology a theology of world history which opened up an indefinite future for the Church.

Let me remark in passing that behind much that is called *Redaktionsgeschichte* there lies the curious assumption that to interpret is to misinterpret. To me it has always seemed a matter of professional prudence on the part of those engaged in interpreting the scriptures to allow for the possibility that an interpreter is sometimes right. It seems to me at least conceivable that Luke, in the interpretation of his sources, has shown how profoundly he understood both the apostolic tradition and the eschatological language in which it came to him.

Having disclosed my bias, I want to examine a number of points at which I believe the modern discussion of eschatology has gone astray. I hope that together they may at least suggest the lines of a persuasive argument, though fully aware that only a Herculean labour could wash away all that I regard as fashionable misconception.

1. The Future

My first point concerns the meaning of the word 'future' and the reference of future verbs in the New Testament. In debates between the advocates of 'realized' and 'futurist' eschatology it has all too often been taken for granted that, if any saying of Jesus could be shown not to apply to the present but to the future, it must be to the absolute future, the End, the parousia, that it refers. As an example let me cite Fuller's treatment of Mark 9:1. 'The event referred to can only be the final coming of the Kingdom . . . Whatever the difficulties, there can be no doubt that it implies the coming of the Kingdom of God as a future event.'[2] To treat 'future' as a synonym for 'final' is not only a *non sequitur*; it is to overlook Mark's use of a verb in the perfect tense. The perfect is normally used to connote completed action with continuing effects in the present, and we need powerful reasons before we assume it to be used otherwise. The Marcan saying undoubtedly *implies* that from the point of view of Jesus the coming of the Kingdom with power is a future event, but what it *states* is that the time will come when some of the bystanders will look back on it as a past event. Whatever it was that Jesus expected, it was to happen in the course of history, not at the end of it.

To this it may be objected that Matthew took 'future' to mean 'final'; for his version of the saying is 'before they see the Son of man coming in his kingdom'. But we had better not use this as a key to the interpretation of Mark unless we are quite sure that we understand what Matthew believed about the coming of the Son of man. For this is not the only passage where he has edited Mark. To Mark 14:62 ('You will see the Son of man seated at the right hand of Power, and coming with the clouds of heaven') Matthew has added the words ἀπ' ἄρτι, 'from now on'. For him the coming of the Son of man with the clouds of heaven was not an event reserved for the Last Day, but one which would begin to happen from the crucifixion onwards, i.e. in the course of history.

I have just pointed out how important it is in dealing with verbs in the future tense to establish from whose standpoint the action is future. At the risk of labouring the obvious, I propose to illustrate this from the Epistle to the Hebrews. The author tells us that his theme is 'the world to come' (τὴν οἰκουμένην τὴν μέλλουσαν). But we should seriously mistake his meaning if we imagined that for him this world was still future. We do not indeed see all things subject to man, but we do see Jesus crowned with glory and honour as the pioneer and representative of his many brothers. Christians have tasted the powers of the age to come and have reached Mount Zion, the city whose architect and builder is God. This author uses the verb μέλλειν with all its future implications because he is thinking of the new age from the point of view of the Old Testament which predicted it. 'The law had a shadow of the good things which were to come' (τῶν μελλόντων ἀγαθῶν) (10:1; cf. 9:11). Similarly Paul can say that Adam was 'the type of him who was to come' (τύπος τοῦ μέλλοντος), future from the point of view of Adam, but not from that of Paul and his fellow-Christians.

This question of standpoint becomes very important when we return to the Gospels to consider some of the sayings of Jesus about judgement. 'It shall be more tolerable on that day for Sodom than for that town' (Luke 10:12). 'It shall be more tolerable in the judgement for Tyre and Sidon than for you' (Luke 10:14). The interpretation of these verses has been dictated by the obvious fact that the only assize in which the people of Sodom, Phoenicia, and Galilee could appear together in the dock is the Last Judgement. It is true that nothing is said here about imminence. Nevertheless, these are passages which have regularly been used as evidence that for Jesus the only future was the ultimate future. Yet on two counts this interpretation must be judged implausible. In any passage of the New Testament which unquestionably deals with the Last Judgement, this is the occasion on which individual destinies are decided: 'They were judged, each man on the record of his deeds' (Rev. 20:13, NEB). But here we have a judgement on towns. Moreover, there is a principle of law that no one shall be put on trial twice for the same offence, and God's judgement on Sodom belongs to the past. 'Remember Sodom and Gomorrah and the neighbouring towns . . . they paid the penalty in eternal fire, an example for all to see' (Jude 7, NEB; cf. 2 Pet. 2:6). 'As things were in Lot's day, also: they ate and drank; they bought and sold; they planted and built; but the day that Lot went out from Sodom, it rained fire and sulphur from the sky and made an end of them all – it will be like that on the day when the Son of Man is revealed' (Luke 17:28–30, NEB). The suggestion that there is a future judgement awaiting the cities of the Plain or the cities of Phoenicia, which have already been destroyed in the past, is nothing more than a trick of syntax. Greek has no future-perfect tense, and the simple future must do service for both. 'It will have been more bearable for Sodom . . .'; that is to say, the past judgement on Sodom will turn out to have been more bearable than the coming judgement on the towns of Galilee. What this comparison meant on the lips of Jesus would have been obvious to anyone who knew the Old Testament. 'The punishment of my people is worse than the penalty of Sodom, which was overthrown in a moment and no one wrung his hands' (Lam. 4:6, NEB). The author of Lamentations envies the people of Sodom because their doom was swift, unheralded, merciful, and complete, unlike the long-drawn-out agonies of Jerusalem under Babylonian siege, in which 'those who died by the sword were more fortunate than those who died of hunger' (Lam. 4:9, NEB).

It may be worth while to remark in passing that this same chapter of Lamentations contains the sentence: 'Our end drew near, our days were numbered, for our end had come' which the Septuagint renders, ῎Ηγγικεν ὁ καιρὸς ἡμῶν, ἐπληρώθησαν αἱ ἡμέραι ἡμῶν, πάρεστιν ὁ καιρὸς ἡμῶν. The similarity between this verse and Mark 1:15 is very striking, and yet it is never so much as mentioned in the arguments by which advocates of futurist eschatology have undertaken to prove that the perfect tense ἤγγικεν must refer to the future.

It is of course proper to respond that Jesus may have used

Old Testament words and images to express ideas different from those of the context in which he found them. It is possible that he believed in a God who at the Last Judgement would inflict prolonged suffering on unbelievers in comparison with which the quick doom of Sodom would seem preferable. What is beyond doubt, however, is that Luke at least understood Jesus' predictions of judgement otherwise, and classified them with the Old Testament prophecies which they closely resembled. In a series of passages which are peculiar to his Gospel he portrays Jesus warning Jerusalem of the imminence of a divine retribution, to be executed by Roman armies, in which all the horrors of 586 BC would be re-enacted (19:41–4; 21:20–4; 23:27–31), with particularly gruesome consequences for pregnant women and the mothers of small children. This was the fate worse than that of Sodom which lay in store for the cities of Galilee if they rejected the proclamation of the Kingdom, because, like Jerusalem, they had failed to recognize the day when God was visiting his people or to know what made for their peace. I am suggesting that there is good reason to think that Luke's interpretation of Jesus was right.

What then are we to make of other passages in which Jesus speaks of judgement? 'The men of Nineveh will arise at the judgement with this generation and condemn it; for they repented at the preaching of Jonah, and behold, something greater than Jonah is here. The queen of the South will arise at the judgement with this generation and condemn it; for she came from the ends of the earth to hear the wisdom of Solomon, and behold, something greater than Solomon is here' (Matt. 12:41–2; Luke 11:31–2). On this passage Kümmel has commented: 'The judgement which will then be held will extend over the whole of mankind. Consequently it presupposes the general resurrection of the dead . . . Since Jesus speaks here of the rising up of "this generation" also, it is clearly expected that at least many of Jesus' contemporaries will die before the rising up and the judgement come. This confirms the fact established by Mark 9:1 that Jesus expected the coming of the *eschaton* to be at hand but not yet very near.'³ Thus are theological silk purses made out of linguistic sows' ears. Matthew and Luke agree in using ἐγείρω in the one instance and ἀνίστημι in the other, and these two verbs are used regularly and interchangeably of the Resurrection. But both verbs are also used in a considerable variety of other senses, both can mean simply 'to appear', and one of them is almost a technical term for a witness appearing in court to give evidence (Mark 14:57). It is in this sense and this sense alone that the verbs are being used in the passage under consideration. No reference to the general resurrection or to the Last Judgement can be intended. For at the Last Judgement all alike will be on trial. But in the present context the Ninevites and the Queen of Sheba are to appear as witnesses for the prosecution at the trial of 'this generation'. The use of courtroom imagery in descriptions of the administration of divine justice in the daily life of men and nations is so frequent in both Testaments that it should hardly be necessary to illustrate it. Job's confidence that after his death his *go'el*, his defence counsel, will stand up in court to vindicate his good name against all charges implies no belief in an after-life for him. In the Fourth Gospel John the Baptist is summoned as a witness in God's lawsuit with the world without having to be raised from the dead to give his evidence. Above all, there is the court scene in Daniel. 'Thrones were set in place and one ancient in years took his seat . . . The court sat, and the books were opened' (Dan. 7:9–10, NEB). Let it be granted that the author of Revelation borrowed and adapted this imagery for his own picture of the Last Judgement (Rev. 20:11–15). No such idea, however, was in the mind of the author of Daniel. His courtroom scene, as he explicitly tells us, is set in the midst of world history. The case before the court is an appeal from the plaintiff Israel, symbolized by the human figure coming on the clouds of heaven, for redress against the tyrannical treatment she has received at the hands of successive world empires, symbolized by the four monsters from the sea. Judgement is given in favour of the saints of the Most High, the last of the pagan kings is stripped of his imperial power, and world sovereignty passes, by legal confiscation, to the nation he has tried to exterminate. In a previous chapter the author has already explained that Nebuchadnezzar was subjected to a particularly humiliating psychosomatic disorder to teach him that 'the Most High is sovereign over the kingdom of men and gives it to whom he will' (4:25, 32, NEB). The attributes which Nebuchadnezzar acquired during his grass-eating phase (nails like eagles' talons) prepare us for the similar characteristics of the first monster in the night visions. The divine court of appeal, we are to understand, keeps close watch over the corruptions of imperial power, and in due course removes it from those who abuse it with bestial cruelty in order to bestow it on those capable of wielding it with humanity. The day of the Son of man in Daniel is the day when God vindicates his elect by giving judgement against their oppressors. So too in the teaching of Jesus the day of judgement is the day when God will vindicate the sons of the Kingdom by convicting their oppressors, even though those oppressors turn out to be not the gentile Romans, but the last generation of the old Israel, obstinately refusing to recant and disown the entail of sin inherited from their fathers. It is entirely compatible with the biblical use of law-court imagery that the sentence of the court should be carried out by human agents.

2. *Token-words*

My second point concerns the use of what Ronald Knox called 'token-words'. Words become tokens when they are regarded as coinage with a uniform and invariable rate of exchange. Knox was attacking that schoolboy method of translation which, through the astonishing advocacy of J. B. Lightfoot, became the basis of the Revised Version, the method of rendering each Hebrew or Greek word by the same word in English in every context in which it occurs. '*Tsedeq* or *dikaiosyne* can mean, when used of man, innocence, or honesty, or uprightness, or charitableness, or dutifulness, or (very commonly) the fact of being in God's good books. Used of God, it can mean the justice which punishes the sinner, or, quite often, the faithfulness which protects the good: it can mean, also, the approval with which God looks upon those who are in his good books. Only a meaningless token-word, like righteousness, can pretend to cover all these meanings. To use such a token-word is to abrogate your duty as a translator.'[4]

It is not my purpose to discuss the relative merits of different translations of the Bible, but simply to point out that the token-word mentality has had a considerable influence on the study of biblical eschatology. We have already seen two excellent examples of it in the first part of this essay. If Jesus ever used the word 'judgement' of the final assize, then by token-word logic that determines its reference in every other context of his teaching. If Jesus said that the Queen of Sheba would rise, she can do no other than rise from the dead. By the same logic it has been argued that, since Jesus on two occasions said that the harvest was ripe for the reapers, therefore in all his parables of growth the present must be equated with the arrival of harvest. It would be interesting to see this homogenizing process applied, for example, to the birds of the air in the two parables of the sower and the mustard seed.

The fact on which Knox was relying, and on which the whole of modern linguistic study is founded, is that all words have multiple meanings; and images are certainly not less multivocal than other forms of language. One would have thought that the relevance of this would have been obvious to all who have studied the phrases 'the kingdom of

God' and 'the Son of man'. For all treatments of these themes in the Gospels begin with an enumeration of the possible senses provided by the Hebrew and Aramaic background. Yet after this promising beginning, we are always asked to decide which *one* of these senses can be ascribed to Jesus. In the Old Testament, God is eternally king; in a more limited sense, he is king over Israel in so far as, within the covenant bond, Israel acknowledges his royal authority; and in a third sense, his reign belongs to the eschatological future. How often have we been told that it is only in this third sense that the New Testament speaks of the Kingdom? Even then, there are further restrictions to be made. Is the Kingdom present or future? Is it a reign or a realm? Is it a state of mind or a state of affairs? The very fact that these questions can be asked at all should be sufficient indication that it is all of these things and more besides. The kingdom of God in the teaching of Jesus is a many-sided concept, and only the context can tell us which aspect of it was uppermost in his mind at any one time. In particular, the classification of the Kingdom as an eschatological concept does not sever its connection with history and politics or diminish the unique role which Israel was expected to play in the realization of God's world-wide sovereignty.

Even more conspicuously has the phrase 'Son of man' been treated as a token. If Jesus ever used the expression, he must have meant exactly the same thing by it every time he used it. Did he say, 'Everyone who acknowledges me before men, the Son of man will acknowledge before the angels of God'? Then those sayings which refer to his ministry or to his passion, and in which the Son of man is identified in whole or in part with himself, cannot be authentic. But why not? If Paul can use the word 'head' in two different senses in a single sentence, there is no obvious reason why Jesus should not use 'Son of man' in two different senses on two different occasions.

In his book *Jesus and the Son of Man*,[5] A. J. B. Higgins

repudiates all the possible Old Testament sources of the
title in favour of the hypothesis that the Similitudes of Enoch
enshrine an apocalyptic tradition of a heavenly redeemer
which is older than Daniel, and from which Daniel's corporate interpretation is a freakish aberration. He cannot,
however, explain away the weighty evidence that the early
Church linked the title both with Psalm 8 and with Daniel 7.
Outside the Gospels, the one is quoted in Hebrews (and
frequently alluded to elsewhere), the other in Revelation. In
the one case Jesus is seen as the fulfilment of the destiny of
man, in the other as the fulfilment of the destiny of Israel.
The two are far from being incompatible, and there is no
a priori reason why Jesus should not have seen himself in both
roles.

Let us suppose for a moment that the Gospels are correct
in representing Daniel 7 as at least the main source of this
title on the lips of Jesus. It would then certainly follow that
T. W. Manson was justified in his corporate interpretation,
i.e. that Jesus used the title of himself, together with any
others who were prepared to share with him the role of
saints of the Most High, through whom God's sovereignty
was to be implemented in the world. Jesus would not thereby
have been debarred from speaking also, without particular
reference to himself or to anyone else, of a day of the Son of
man, when the heavenly court would sit and vindicate the
sons of the Kingdom by pronouncing sentence on those who
had rejected both them and the Gospel. Please note that I
do not for one moment claim that by this brief argument I
have proved this to be the case. My sole concern is to expose
the fatuity of arguments which purport to demonstrate that
it is not.

3. *The Meaning of Eschatology*

My third point has to do with the meaning of 'eschatology'.
The classical definition of the word is that given in the

Oxford English Dictionary: 'The department of theological science concerned with the four last things: death, judgement, heaven and hell.' In this sense 'eschatology' deals with the ultimate destiny of the individual. Only since the beginning of this century has the word been used in the sense we all now take for granted, to cover the biblical teaching about the destiny of the world and the working out of God's purposes in and through his holy people. This is a perfectly legitimate semantic development, but one which offers ample opportunity for confusion and logical fallacy. It has generally been assumed that 'eschatology' in this second sense deals with the *eschaton*, the End; and that the End entails the same degree of finality for the historic process as death does for the individual. But a glance at a concordance shows us that this is by no means always true. The end which Amos saw, for instance, in his vision of summer fruit was the end of the nation of Israel. Even when the prophets depict the end in terms of cosmic collapse, this is but oriental hyperbole; the end still has a limited national reference.

It was for this reason that Mowinckel denied that the pre-exilic prophets had an eschatology. We may safely agree with him, provided we see clearly what it is that he is doing. He is defining 'eschatology' in such a way that the term becomes irrelevant to the evidence before him. He feels justified in so doing because he believes that his definition does apply to literature of a later period. If the prophets were not interested in the end of the world, at least the apocalyptists were. No longer believing that history was the arena for the mighty acts of God, despairing of human help, they counted the days till the End and the divine intervention it would bring.

I have always been unhappy with this hard-and-fast distinction between prophecy and apocalyptic, partly because apocalyptic characteristics are found in the writings of the prophets, partly because the pejorative description of apocalyptic, whatever support it may gain from the more erratic of the pseudepigrapha, does not fit any of the three apocalyptic writings which attained canonicity. The Book of Daniel is concerned with an historical crisis, the persecution of the Jewish nation by Antiochus Epiphanes. It does, to be sure, make a major contribution to biblical theology by setting that persecution against a backdrop of world history. One of the author's chief pastoral purposes was to assure the beleaguered people that the whole of history is under the control of God. But the only end he evinces any interest in is the end of persecution. 'I said to the man clothed in linen who was above the waters of the river, "How long will it be before these portents cease?" The man clothed in linen above the waters lifted to heaven his right hand and his left, and I heard him swear by him who lives for ever: "It shall be for a time, times, and a half. When the power of the holy people ceases to be dispersed, all these things shall come to an end"' (Dan. 12:6–7, NEB). The Revelation of St John paints the scenery of world history on a larger canvas and in more vivid and more moving colours, yet it too is anchored in contemporary history through the expectation of 'what must soon take place', the persecution of the Church by the totalitarian power of the Roman Empire. In 4 Ezra the crisis is neither present nor future, but past: for the author, as is particularly clear in the Eagle Vision, is grappling with the theological implications of Roman imperialism and of the destruction of Jerusalem by the armies of Titus thirty years earlier.

Because of the intractability of the biblical material, prophetic and apocalyptic alike, to any scheme of thoroughgoing eschatology, a new term has been introduced into the debate. What the Jewish people expected was not *Das Ende* but *Die Endzeit*. If this distinction were consistently maintained it would be a very useful one. The difficulty is that it is all too easy to shift one's ground from the one to the other. But to expect an End is not the same as to expect an Endtime. The one is an event beyond which nothing can conceivably happen. The other is a period of indefinite duration in which much is expected to happen.

In S. G. Wilson's monograph, *The Gentiles and the Gentile Mission in Luke–Acts*,[6] an otherwise scholarly and persuasive argument is weakened by neglect of this distinction. Jesus, so the author tells us, did not expect a mission to the Gentiles, because he 'believed that this hope would be fulfilled in the apocalyptic events of the End-time'. Mark retains the eschatological setting of the proclamation to the Gentiles, but sees it as 'a historical process which must be completed before the End comes'. 'Luke makes the final and perhaps inevitable break, by severing even the eschatological connections.' What needs to be questioned here is the contrast, which Dr Wilson is by no means the first to make, between apocalyptic or eschatological events on the one hand and historical events on the other. An unhistorical event is a contradiction in terms, since history in this sense is simply the succession of events, and after history ends there can be no more events. If events happen, even if they are assigned to a period which we choose to call the End-time, they are historical. The careful distinction, therefore, between the expectations of Jesus, Mark and Luke evaporates, and with it Luke's supposed historicizing of an originally eschatological tradition.

The last refuge of the thorough-going eschatologist lies in the assumption that, once the End-time has begun, the End itself must be just round the corner. But this inference is neither logically entailed nor supported by the evidence. When Daniel sees the court in session, judgement given in favour of the Son of man, and world sovereignty passing to the saints of the Most High, he tells us that their kingdom is an everlasting kingdom. If this is the *Endzeit*, it is of unlimited duration. If there is one phrase which better than any sums up the biblical view of the future, it is 'for ever and ever' (εἰς τους αἰῶνας τῶν αἰώνων). It is perhaps plausible that the early Christians were so deeply conscious of having experienced in Christ, in his resurrection, and in the coming of the Spirit, the fulfilment of the Old Testament promises that occasionally, especially in times of apocalyptic crisis, they felt the frontiers of the future close in upon them. But most of the time they lived with the wider horizons of the Old Testament hopes on which their faith was nourished. In the earliest book of the New Testament Paul is already assuring his friends in Thessalonica that they need have no anxiety about the coming of the Day, they who are now sons of light. Seventy years later the author of 2 Peter is giving his readers the same assurance, because one day or a thousand years are all the same in the patient purposes of God.

I am painfully conscious that I have here presented neither a thesis nor the skeleton of a thesis, but only a few scattered bones. But I trust they are enough to suggest the possibilities of articulation and to justify the suggestion of my title that what we call eschatology has at least as much to do with the politics of the people of God as with expectations of an End, and that the biblical librarians would do well to take a fresh look at their cataloguing system.

North and South: Tension and Reconciliation in Biblical History

Charles H. H. Scobie

Every student of biblical history knows that on the death of Solomon the ten Northern tribes broke away and formed a separate 'Northern Kingdom', Judah and Benjamin alone being faithful to the house of David and continuing as the 'Southern Kingdom'.[1] Thus the ancient unity of God's people was broken. The fall of the Northern Kingdom to the Assyrians in 722 BC made the split final and in fact eliminated the Northerners as a component part of the people of God. The Northern population was deported and replaced by foreigners from whom were descended the Samaritans, the 'Kuthim' and 'lion-converts'[2] of Jewish tradition, racially impure and religiously syncretistic.

This account, based on the Old Testament, Josephus and Rabbinic sources, has long been the generally accepted view of North-South relations. In relatively recent times, however, a very different assessment has come to light through the study of the literature of the Samaritans.[3] The Samaritans claim to be of pure (Northern) Israelite descent and pure religion. In their view the original centre of administration and worship was at Shechem in the North and the faith was corrupted when a rival group broke away to establish a new centre at Shiloh and then later at Jerusalem. In particular the Samaritan tradition rejects the developments from the time of David and Solomon onwards which centred the faith at Jerusalem under a monarchy of Davidic descent.

Both Jewish and Samaritan accounts are biased and reflect the history of bitterness and hostility between the two groups. In the picture which is emerging from modern scholarly study it is becoming clear that the tension between North and South is, somewhat paradoxically, both much older than the traditional views allow, yet in other respects also later than is commonly supposed.

Jewish and Samaritan histories are based on the Pentateuch, which undoubtedly idealizes the early history of Israel. Recent historical and archaeological studies present a picture of various tribes infiltrating into Palestine over a number of centuries.[4] It is widely accepted that not all the tribes participated in the Exodus experience.[5] From the very beginning there were divisions and rivalries.[6] It was only in the period of the Judges that the various tribes came together and then only in some form of confederation based on a common faith in Yahweh.[7] There may well be truth in the Samaritan claims that Shechem was the centre of such a confederation in the time of Joshua.[8] Political union under David and Solomon was the exception not the rule.

The account in I Kings 12:1–24 of the break-up of the 'united' kingdom is instructive. Solomon's son Rehoboam was accepted as David's successor in the South, but was obliged to go to the ancient Northern centre of Shechem to be made king by the consent of the Northern tribes. His policy statement alienated the North, revived the war-cry of the old tribal confederation, 'To your tents, O Israel',[9] and split the kingdom in two.

After 922 BC Yahwism flourished in the North, despite the dangers of syncretism. Here the 'E' traditions of the Pentateuch took shape; here the prophetic movement began with Elijah and Elisha and flourished with the ministries of Amos and Hosea; here the core of the Deuteronomic traditions took shape.[10] Political division did not mean the closing of the lines of communication at the religious level. When political disaster overtook Samaria we have to suppose that loyal Yahwists carried the Northern traditions, written and oral, to the South.

Recent analyses recognize in 2 Kings 17 a highly biased, Jewish view of Samaritan origins.[11] Deportations did take place but these affected only a small percentage of the population, though they probably included the religious leaders. This must have dealt a serious blow to Yahwism; the measure of the disaster on the religious front is the non-survival of pre-722 BC religious literature in the North.

Many Yahwists must have survived, however. Jeremiah and Ezekiel still know nothing of the view that the Northerners were pagan foreigners. Indeed, as H. H. Rowley has pointed out, while Ezekiel does not question the racial purity of Samaria, he does question that of the Jerusalemites![12] The tensions of the post-exilic period were still political rather than religious.[13] The two communities (or at least some elements within them) were certainly in full communion at least up to the time of the final compilation of the Pentateuch. The building of a Samaritan temple on Mount Gerizim in the time of Alexander the Great,[14] and its destruction by John Hyrcanus in 128 BC were major factors in the final religious separation of the two communities.[15]

This gradual parting of the ways gave shape to rival 'Northern' and 'Southern' theologies. The Southern tradition, for example, became irrevocably tied to *Jerusalem* as the holy city, and a 'Zion theology' was developed.[16] Northern Yahwism could not accept the Zion theology but was able to appeal to the very ancient traditions centring in the Shechem area, 'the navel of the land' (Judg. 9:37).[17]

Connected with this is the place the Jerusalem *Temple* came to occupy in Southern theology; the North countered with claims for a sanctuary on Mount Gerizim hallowed long before the time of David by its association with the Tabernacle.[18]

Equally central in the thought of the South is the place of the Davidic dynasty, which finds its expression in the *Royal*

Theology of 2 Samuel 7 and the royal Psalms. Southern theology reinterpreted the *covenant* as a covenant with the house of David,[19] whereas the North seems to have held more closely to the older covenant conception, perhaps under the influence of covenant renewal festivals.[20] Southern theology may be characterized as *'dynastic'* while the Northern view was more 'democratic' in the sense that charismatic leaders ruled by the consent of the tribes.[21] In the absence of Davidic traditions it is the figure of Moses which tends to be emphasized in the North.

Not surprisingly these tendencies are important in the *eschatological expectations* which developed separately in North and South. Southern eschatology was Jerusalem-centred,[22] while Samaritan theology associated the events of the End-time with Mount Gerizim.[23] The concept of a New Temple is a prominent feature of the Jewish eschatological hope,[24] while Samaritan eschatology looked for a restoration of the Tabernacle.[25] The Southern messianic hope centred in a future Son of David, whereas the typical Northern expectation was a Moses-like prophet as foretold in Deuteronomy 18:15–18.

2

The ancient tension and the gradually widening division between North and South do not tell the whole story; within the prophetic books of the Old Testament there are voices which speak in sympathetic terms of the North and which hope for a reconciliation and a reunion of God's people as part of the general eschatological hope.

While Jeremiah[26] does not overlook the sins of the North, he speaks of Yahweh's continuing care for her (Jer. 3:12). The 'Book of Comfort' (chapters 30 and 31) assures the North that Yahweh loves her 'with an everlasting love' (Jer. 31:3); Yahweh, the good shepherd, is to gather in his scattered flock (Jer. 31:10); God's people are to make a new start and

North and South will be reunited when Yahweh makes a 'new covenant with the house of Israel and the house of Judah . . .' (Jer. 31:31).

Ezekiel's interest in the North is even more apparent, so that it has actually been argued that he was a Northerner himself.[27] Both North and South have sinned, but Judah is more blameworthy than Israel (Ezek. 16:44f.; 23). Ezekiel's hopes for the future emerge in chapters 33f. Israel has been led astray by false shepherds, but Yahweh will gather in his scattered flock and once again care for his sheep (Ezek. 34); God's people must be inwardly cleansed and renewed (Ezek. 36:25, 26); indeed, God's people must rise from the dead through the inbreathing of God's Spirit (Ezek. 37:1–14). This is the context for the Oracle of the Two Sticks (Ezek. 37:15–23), in which the prophet is instructed to take a stick and write on it 'For Judah', and another stick, to be inscribed 'For Joseph', and to join them together 'that they may become one in your hand', as a symbol of the eschatological reunion of North and South.[28]

The hoped-for reunion of North and South is incorporated into the vision of the New Community and the New Temple in Ezekiel 40–8, for in the ideal future re-allocation of the land (Ezek. 45:1–8; 47:13–48:35) all twelve tribes are to receive equal portions. A striking feature of the allocation of territory is the separation of the sanctuary from the city; if the city is assumed to be on the site of Jerusalem, then the sanctuary which lies further north is not a restored Jerusalem Temple. This has led some scholars to suggest that the sanctuary was located by Ezekiel at Shechem, the ancient capital of the original tribal confederation.[29] Many features of Ezekiel's vision are illuminated by this identification. To give one example, the description of the life-giving stream issuing from the temple fits better the Wâdî Fâr'ah flowing from the Shechem area eastwards to the Jordan valley and then south to the Dead Sea than the conventional identification with the Kidron.[30]

The teaching of Jeremiah and Ezekiel on North and South is virtually unique.[31] The fall of the Northern Kingdom was a great temptation to Judah to see herself as alone the chosen of God. The impending, and then actual, fall of the South evened the score, as it were, so that neither side could vaunt itself. It is in this historical setting that the prophetic mind saw the need for a radical new beginning based on a reconciliation and a reconstruction of the ideal unity of God's people, both North and South.

In subsequent centuries, as relations deteriorated, the teaching of the great prophets was forgotten. The section on the Flock and the Shepherds in (II) Zechariah 11:4–17 is a pessimistic reversal of Ezekiel's Oracle of the Two Sticks, probably prompted by the building of the Gerizim temple;[32] in it the prophet says, 'Then I broke my second staff Union, annulling the brotherhood between Judah and Israel.'

In later Jewish thought there were two main views of the North. According to one view, based on 2 Kings 17, the whole Northern population was deported to a distant land where they still exist.[33] This was combined in some apocalypses, however, with the expectation of their eschatological restoration, a view presumably inspired by the Jeremiah and Ezekiel prophecies.[34] That this hope was by no means universally accepted is testified to by the divided opinions recorded in the Mishnah:

> The Ten Tribes shall not return again, for it is written, *And he cast them into another land like this day* (Deut. 29:28). Like as this day goes and returns not, so do they go and return not. So R. Akiba. But R. Eliezer says: Like as the day grows dark and then grows light, so also after darkness is fallen upon the Ten Tribes shall light thereafter shine upon them.[35]

A second view either does not know or else completely ignores the tradition of the ten tribes living in distant exile; instead, it regards the existing Jewish community as repre-

senting all twelve tribes. This is illustrated by the account of
the translation of the Septuagint given in the Letter of
Aristeas, according to which the translation was made by
seventy-two men sent from Jerusalem, six from each of the
twelve tribes.[36]

3

The early Christian Church, according to the Book of Acts,
began in Jerusalem; the first Christians were all Jews; they
attended the Jerusalem Temple (Acts 2:46; 3:1f.); they
formed a sect within Judaism, distinguished by their recognition of Jesus as the Davidic Messiah (Acts 2:22–36). In
terms of our discussion of North and South, early Christianity
would appear to be thoroughly *Southern* in its origins and
orientation.

Even the Book of Acts, however, which gives a strongly
Jerusalem-centred interpretation of Christian origins, tells
of how some of those dispersed from Jerusalem after the death
of Stephen led the first Christian mission – to Samaria, the
ancient Northern Kingdom![37] These missionaries belonged
to what we may call the Stephen-Philip group (usually
identified with the 'Hellenists' of Acts 6), in contrast to
what we may call the Peter-James group (usually identified
with the 'Hebrews'). The Stephen-Philip group was responsible for a missionary outreach in which *three stages* can
be discerned: firstly, a mission to *Jews* (Acts 11:19), secondly
to *Samaritans* (Acts 8), and thirdly to *Gentiles* (Acts 11:20).

Important as this Stephen-Philip movement thus is, we
know surprisingly little about it. Acts 6:1–6 contains a
minimum of historical information; Acts 6:8–15; 7:54–8:1
appears to be based on a Martyrdom of Stephen, edited by
Luke, into which has been inserted the speech of Stephen
(Acts 7:2–53).[38] New light has been shed on the Samaritan
mission by the recognition that Stephen's speech is based on
a source which employs readings found in the Samaritan

Pentateuch, incorporates Samaritan traditions and view-points, and in its use of Old Testament texts betrays a Samaritan or Northern bias.[39] Rather than being an accurate transcript of what Stephen actually said, the speech source is best explained as a product of the Samaritan mission of Acts 8. Though he had access to some good source material, Luke himself has only a hazy idea of the connection between events at this period and it is easy to understand how he ascribed this source to Stephen though historically it represents a development which did not occur until after Stephen's death.[40]

The Samaritan mission indicates that the Stephen-Philip group did not share either of the two main views of the North found in contemporary Judaism. Rather, they apparently accepted the Samaritans as part of God's people and sought to share with them the good news of the fulfilment of God's purposes for Israel. This strongly suggests that the group had *Northern* interests and sympathies which were not found in contemporary main-line Judaism.

It is a speculation, but not an irresponsible one, that the prophecies of Jeremiah and Ezekiel were utilized by this group. It is one of the surprises of the New Testament that nowhere is Ezekiel's prophecy of the outpouring of the Spirit (Ezek. 37:1–14) directly alluded to.[41] Since this passage is directly followed by the Oracle of the Two Sticks (Ezek. 37:15–23), foretelling the reunion of North and South, it is an attractive thesis that Philip's group, finding in Ezekiel 37 a *testimonium* relating to the outpouring of the Spirit, found there also the justification for their mission to the North. Since the prophecy of the New Covenant (Jer. 31:31–4) was used in the early Church,[42] it also may have been an influence with its reference to 'a new covenant with the house of Israel and the house of Judah'.

These indications of *Northern* sympathies on the part of the Stephen-Philip group are confirmed especially when the group is compared with the 'Hebrews', led by Peter and then by James, who clearly exhibit *Southern* characteristics.[43]

(a) Following Jesus' resurrection, James apparently went to *Jerusalem* (Gal. 1:19; Acts 1:13); there he remained and rose to be leader of the community (Gal. 2:9; Acts 15; 21:18f.). James, Peter and the other Galileans presumably went to Jerusalem because their theology was basically Southern: they went to await the eschatological events which would take place in the holy city! The Stephen-Philip group on the other hand were driven from Jerusalem and the city plays no part in their thought.

(b) Similarly, the Peter-James group frequented the Jerusalem *Temple*,[44] whereas Stephen spoke against it (Acts 6:13–14), and the speech source of Acts 7 is violently anti-Temple (7:44f.).

(c) Again, it appears that the Peter-James group favoured a Davidic *Christology*, if Acts 2:25–35 is in any way an accurate reflection of early Christian preaching in Jerusalem.[45] Davidic Christology is notably absent in Stephen's speech, where the Moses-like prophet is the key category.[46] The Martyrdom source connects a Son of man Christology with Stephen in a unique reference at Acts 7:56 which suggests that the exalted Christ has been assigned the role of Moses as the one who stands before God and intercedes for his people.[47]

(d) Particularly interesting is the way James came to assume the leadership of the Jerusalem community; this was undoubtedly due to his relationship to Jesus. Here we have a *dynastic* principle in operation (cf. the Moslem caliphate), as is shown by the choice, upon the death of James, of Symeon, a cousin of Jesus, as his successor.[48] The leadership remains in the Davidic succession. The election of the Seven in Acts 6, on the other hand, is strongly reminiscent of the Northern practice of charismatic leaders ruling by the consent of the people.

All this invites us to see in the Stephen-Philip group a

type of *Northern*, sectarian Judaism, represented within the Christian community from the very beginning. As the group under Peter, and particularly James, developed along Southern theological lines, the Northern group, forced to flee from Jerusalem, turned naturally to Samaria. With this mission, they believed, the eschatological reunion of God's people (North and South) had begun. When this was seen to be so, the next step became logical: the time for the eschatological ingathering of the Gentiles was also here! The Stephen-Philip group thus played a key role in the development of Christianity from a sect of Judaism into a universal religion.

4

Strong Northern sympathies are clearly apparent in the Gospel of John. While Jesus gathers some followers from among the Jews of Jerusalem, it is there that he is largely rejected by 'his own'.[49] On the other hand, it is in Samaria that Jesus reveals himself as the Messiah (John 4:25–6), is hailed as 'the Saviour of the world' (John 4:42), and 'many' believe in him (John 4:39, 41). John's Gospel, in fact, represents the viewpoint of the Stephen-Philip movement in its first two (Jewish, Samaritan) stages but not yet its third (Gentile) stage. The *Temple* is replaced by a new form of worship; Davidic *Christology* is rejected but Mosaic themes are dominant; the role of *Peter and James* is played down.[50]

This approach to the Gospel sheds light for example on John 10:1–18, in which the image of the sheep and the shepherd reflects the influence especially of Jeremiah and Ezekiel. Jesus is presented as 'the good shepherd' (John 10:11), a figure who usually corresponds in the Old Testament either to Yahweh himself, [51] or to a messianic, Davidic shepherd-king.[52] Here, as elsewhere in John, it is striking how the Davidic Christological motif is avoided. John 10:3–4, on the other hand, clearly reflects Numbers 27:15–23, where *Moses* appoints a successor to take over his function as shepherd.

The passage further picks up the theme of the scattering and ingathering of the flock. The wolf scatters the sheep (10:12), whereas the good shepherd will gather in the 'other sheep' so that 'there shall be one flock, one shepherd' (10:16).[53] Despite the usual interpretation, there is no justification for regarding the 'other sheep' as Gentiles.[54] Following J. Bowman,[55] we note that the passages in Jeremiah and Ezekiel reflected here are those closely connected with the reunion of North and South. The concept of the 'one shepherd' in particular (Ezek. 37:24) comes directly after the Oracle of the Two Sticks (Ezek. 37:15–23) which foretells the reunion of Judah and Israel. In John 10 Jesus speaks to Jerusalem Jews (cf. 9:40; 10:19), and his 'own sheep' are those Jews who believe in him; the 'other sheep' are the Samaritans whose ingathering has been anticipated in John 4.[56] What is envisaged is the reconstituting of the true Israel, North and South.

Allusions to Ezekiel and (II) Zechariah also shed light on the references to 'living water' in John 4:10–15 and 7:37–9. John 7:38 raises a problem: 'He who believes in me, as the scripture has said, "Out of his belly shall flow rivers of living water."' No known scripture passage corresponds with this quotation, but the most probable reference is to the concept of the life-giving river issuing from the holy mountain and from the new temple at the centre or navel of the earth.[57] Later interpreters certainly understood Ezekiel to refer to Jerusalem ('On that day living waters shall flow out from Jerusalem': Zech. 14:8), but the rival Northern view associated the tradition with the Shechem area. Now it is interesting that Christ as the source of the eschatological living water occurs in *two* passages in John's Gospel. (a) In John 4: 10–15, in Samaria, the water Jesus gives is contrasted with the water of Jacob's well, the water which comes from the centre of the earth according to Northern tradition.

(b) In John 7:37–9, Jesus offers living water in Jerusalem, the source of the eschatological river according to Southern tradition. Here again we see a combining of Northern and Southern theologies, though it is not simply a case of Jesus fulfilling both sets of expectations. The new reality brought by Jesus transcends both expectations: the eschatological river of life flows neither from Mount Gerizim nor from Mount Zion, but is to be found in Christ himself.[58]

5

It is possible that the Stephen-Philip movement has left one other trace in the New Testament, for affinities have been found between Samaritan thought and the Epistle to the Hebrews.[59] It is unlikely that the writer of the Epistle was a Samaritan Christian but it is possible that the *recipients* were a small group (such as a house church) of Samaritan Christians, within a larger Jewish-Christian community. As in Acts 7 and John's Gospel, Davidic Christology is rejected,[60] though the writer also regards a Mosaic Christology (favoured by the readers of the letter?) as inadequate,[61] and proceeds to expound his own highly original Christology. As in John's Gospel, there is absolutely no mention of a Gentile mission and it may well be the first two (Jewish, Samaritan) stages of the Stephen-Philip outreach which are represented here. This would give particular point to the writer's emphasis on Jeremiah's New Covenant. The eschatological reunion of God's people may be in his mind when he quotes Jeremiah 31:31–4 in full (Heb. 8:8–12), including the reference to 'a new covenant with the house of Israel and with the house of Judah'.

The theme of tension and reconciliation between North and South may thus be traced throughout biblical history, shedding new light not only on Old Testament themes but also on the origins and development of the community of the New Covenant.

The Epistle for Today

Neil Alexander

We speak of 'an idea whose time has come', 'a tract for the times', 'the man for the hour'. This essay takes 'The Epistle for Today' in a similar sense: as that New Testament epistle with pre-eminent claim to be called *the* epistle for our time. We shall be asking which it is and why.

THE EPISTLES FOR TODAY

Some readers would stop us before we start. 'Why bother with any Epistle any time? We have the Gospels with their timeless saving story. What more do we need? The Epistles, too, are obscure and difficult; they only muddy what in the Gospels is crystal clear. Besides, does not Paul in his letters actually distort the simple message of Jesus in the Gospels, transforming it into a Christianity Jesus would have disowned? We've heard experts say so. All in all, we're surely better off without the Epistles!'

Along such lines the Epistles are commonly disparaged. In rebuttal and in preface to our enquiry, we feel bound to 'put in a word' for the Epistles as a whole. It can only be brief and over-simplifying but some *apologia* is clearly needed, especially for the Epistles *vis-à-vis* the Gospels.

The experts' charge against Paul, an old one, continues to be made, but its unfairness has in our time been convincingly demonstrated by other experts, at least as notable. Properly appraised, Paul is no fabricator. His gospel is the Gospel.

Those above who are so critical of Paul and the Epistles are, further, naïvely *un*critical of the Gospels. For them, apparently, 'the Gospels with their timeless saving story' are problem-free – which they are not. It is fair to claim that they do tell essentially the same saving story, the Gospel, but there are four tellings. In many points these disagree: Which has 'the truth'? Why do they disagree? Because not all the evangelists have had access to the same 'facts'? More often because (as merest scratching below the Gospels' surface shows) not a single evangelist is a so-called plain historian ('confining himself to the facts'): all are interpreters, editors, ecclesiastics and theologians. As much potential for distortion must, therefore, be ascribed to them as to theologian Paul! Study certainly does not support the popular assumption that there is some 'special' quality of original simplicity and pristine purity in the Gospels. (It may be there to be discovered but it cannot be assumed.) Perhaps if this myth were dispelled, its corollary would also go: that the Epistles are 'not in the same class' and 'rather a come-down after the Gospels!'

This 'after' is unfortunately true to uninformed popular belief – confirmed, of course, by the 'Gospels . . . Epistles' order in our printed Bible. A tragic error! It hides one of the great glories of the Epistles: the earliness of so many of them. All Paul's authentic letters (ten, if we include Ephesians) – and perhaps Hebrews and 1 Peter as well – antedate even the earliest of the four Gospels (Mark, AD 67). They take us, through 'received' material in the letters (e.g. 1 Cor. 11:23–6; 15:3ff.) and the pre-Pauline hymns in Philippians 2:6–11 and Ephesians 5:14, right to the threshold of 'that which was from the beginning' in Christian belief, preaching and worship. The earliest Epistles, the first complete Christian writings, Galatians and 1 and 2 Thessalonians (AD 49–51), are at no more than two decades' distance from the Crucifixion and the Resurrection. Are the Gospels, then, to be discounted? Not at all. Despite their relative lateness, they are absolutely indispensable. They alone fill out for us, in considerable detail, through narrative and teaching, the amazing story of Jesus Christ Incarnate which the Epistles only presuppose, allude to, at most summarily rehearse. The claim upon us of the Epistles' own content, however, is no less commanding, and their exhilarating freshness, springing from birth, in most cases, in the Church's dawn, makes the study of the Epistles peculiarly rewarding.

Words on the jacket of volume II of Professor Barclay's New Testament translation[1] are much to the point. 'The Letters are of the greatest importance for it is in them, and in them alone, that we can trace the development of the Church and the Church's life and faith in the earliest days. In them we meet practical problems of life and conduct, and the even deeper problems presented by those who attacked and those who perverted the faith.' In them, translated in such a way as to be *interpreted*, 'modern man may find, not only information about the past, but also guidance for the present'.

The 'blurb' on this excellent volume also says, somewhat in line with the popular plaint which necessitated this preface, 'There is no part of the New Testament harder for a modern man to understand than the Letters.' The reason given is, 'The Gospels are narrative; the Letters are argument; and argument is always more difficult to follow than narrative.' (Difficulties involving words and ideas, however, can be overcome by resort to an *interpretative* translation (such as Professor Barclay's) and to commentaries. For understanding even the Gospels these are helpful; for understanding the Epistles they are obligatory.) In such respects the Epistles *are* undoubtedly harder than the Gospels to understand.

On another, deeper, level of understanding – the level of feeling 'at home' and *en rapport* – the position is reversed! We make bold to say that it is vastly easier for modern man (especially if he has done the indicated obligatory homework) to identify with the world of the Epistles than with the world of the Gospels. For three reasons: (a) Our world, like that of the Epistles, is entirely *post-Crucifixion, post-Resurrection*. With how much reality can we 'archaize' ourselves today into a time setting and world setting such as those of the Gospels, in which (for most of the Gospels' length) the Crucifixion and the Resurrection are, ostensibly, 'not yet'? (b) Our world, like the Epistles', is entirely *post-Pentecost*. That is, it is a world in which the Christian Church, as an organization of distinctive power and activity, is an established fact and significant ongoing social factor. Even if we do not belong to the Church, this is our world today! If we do belong, as members or ministers of a congregation, we have an immediate connection with the Epistles (to which the Gospels can offer no rival parallel). It is made in the moment when the elementary truth strikes home that these letters are addressed to, and relate to the life of, the *Church* at Corinth, the Christian *congregations* in Galatia, Philippi, etc. They speak with the greatest directness and relevance to us whose life also is church life, congregational life, in this post-Pentecost world. The Epistles' *locus* is ours. (c) Our world, like the Epistles' world, is *outside first-century Palestine*. The religious world of first-century Palestine is recreated for us with (so far as we can judge) remarkable fidelity by the Evangelists – the Synoptists certainly, but also, in the main, John. The world of the Gospels emerges as a world of diversified Judaism (e.g. Galilean, Pharisaic, Sadducean, Essene, Zealot, 'unscrupulous' and indifferent). Multiform Judaism, but always – and only – *Judaism*! Even the most revolutionary words and deeds of Jesus, far from springing from any religious influence alien to Judaism, come from the passion to be the true Jew, to bring Judaism to its true fulfilment, to form with his disciples the true Israel. The Evangelists, rightly, never for a moment represent Roman or Greek cults or philosophies, higher or lower Hellenistic paganism, as active challenges to Palestinian Judaism and credible live options confronting the people of

Jehovah. Rightly, because such conditions did not obtain. The world of the Gospels – i.e. of first-century Palestine – is, in today's jargon, a religiously simplistic society.

This is just not our world at all today! In the days of medieval Christendom, probably it was. In several countries (including Scotland), within their own bounds, somewhat similar conditions existed again in the immediate post-Reformation era. With the rise of rationalism, nationalism, and the new religions of the sciences and pseudo-sciences, however, such a situation vanished long ago. Recent years in our society have brought, too, a host of further religions into sight and, in some instances, into prominence and proselytizing power – such as Satanism and Scientology, anti-materialist Hippyism and *La Dolce Vita* Hedonism, Bahai and Buddhism and Mohammedanism. Today, beyond question, we live in a spiritually, or religiously, pluralistic society which bears no resemblance whatever to the world of the Gospels. Just as beyond question is it that our world today is strikingly, excitingly like the pluralistic first-century Greco-Roman society – outside of Palestine – in which the Epistles live and move and have their being. (To appreciate this we no doubt need to read up a little about Stoicism and Epicureanism, about the Gnostic movement and the mystery religions and other powerful influences of the period and area, but the background material is within easy, readable reach. And no one has done more than Professor Barclay to put it there!)

The Epistles' setting is a society in which Christians were in a minority, a despised minority, battered on all sides by anti-Christian forces, urgently obliged to think out where they stood and how to relate themselves to the essentially pagan (if also, often, 'religious') majority-world around them; a minority working out, for life and action, what in their situation the Gospel was, what their commitment and commission entailed, and how best they could communicate their faith to the hostile, sceptical, indifferent, to those of

other faiths and philosophies and those of none. That is the
Epistles' world. Ours too.

'Why any Epistle any day? Why bother with the Epistles
at all?' In the light of what has been outlined, we conclude:
We simply cannot do without the Epistles. We never could.
But more than ever, by the almost uncanny mirroring of our
world in theirs, they have claim upon our study and esteem.
It may not be too much to say that they are *the* New Testament scriptures for today.

THE EPISTLE FOR TODAY

We go on now to our major task – controversial and admit-
tedly subjective – of selecting *the* Epistle for today. We do
not select it, however, without prior acknowledgement that
each of the *un*selected Epistles remains *an* Epistle for today.
Though it may be through only a single paragraph (e.g.
2 Thess. 3:6–13), even a single memorable sentence (e.g.
Jude 24), every Epistle – however 'low in the charts' for
today it may seem as a whole – speaks valuably still; if not
to us personally, to someone, we may be sure, somewhere
on the globe. No 'blind spot', no idiosyncracy of ours, should
make us dismiss *any* of the Epistles as being unserviceable
today. Take James! We confess we would be happy if you
took James – and we would have Luther's support. Yet
Erik Routley[2] writes of Luther on James: 'How anybody
could regard as "negligible" a document which so uniquely
reflects, in the ongoing context of the early Church, the
authentic teaching of Christ as we have it in the Gospels, I
have yet to discover; perhaps one day he [Luther presum-
ably] will tell me. Until then I value James as much as I
value anything after Romans in the New Testament.' We are
rebuked, for clearly James – like every other canonical
Epistle – can be extremely precious to contemporary
readers attuned to it. It, like all, is at least *an* Epistle for
today.

But *the* Epistle? Here we have right and reason to be selective. The tiny Epistles Philemon, 2 and 3 John, Jude, for example, offer too meagre a diet, obviously, for any one of them to be pre-eminently *the* Epistle for our time. 'Out', too, go the brief letters to the Thessalonians and 2 Peter: their obsession with primitive eschatology precludes their being today's choice. Despite Erik Routley's commendation of James – and noting that it is not even *his* pre-eminent Epistle – we let James go: it lacks the theological richness we can find elsewhere. It will be generally agreed that we should dismiss the Pastorals. However helpful many of their contents do prove to many today, these letters as a whole so lack *élan* and are so out of sympathy with change that they rule themselves out as the epistolary 'Word for the Seventies': it is not with their style of answer that we successfully cope with 'Future Shock'!

Philippians, too, is not a serious candidate for the post of *the* Epistle. While its notes of joy and hope match and support our contemporary theological mood admirably and while Philippians 2:5–11 (the *kenosis* passage) has power to grip modern laymen as well as theologians, the letter is, overall, too slight theologically, and too personal, for our purpose; marred, also, by its savagely controversial portions at the beginning and end of chapter 3.

Galatians we take the liberty of eliminating undiscussed, on one simple ground: that what Galatians gives us is more roundedly given, and given better 'for today', in Romans.

It is time to clarify what we mean by 'for today' in 'The Epistle for Today'. We understand it as a combination of 'most wanted today', i.e. most desired and willingly received, and 'most needed today', i.e. needed for our good, whether we like it or not! By 'most wanted' we mean the Epistle most nearly on today's man's mental wave-length; the one which understands his basic needs in terms most readily meaningful to him, which has insights which 'today's people' seem aptest to grasp and accept. By 'most needed' we mean the Epistle most challengingly corrective of those tendencies in our present-day society – and Church – which are seen, by Christian critique, to be most seriously harmful and sinful.

We seek the Epistle which best combines these qualities. It must also be one which has no fatal *contra*-indication of suitability as '*The* Epistle for Today'.[3]

The first Epistle of John has good points of claim 'for today': for example its abhorrence of the hypocrisy that would permit a gulf between profession and practice; the weight it gives to love (*agape*); its being, indeed, the one place in the New Testament in which to find explicitly 'God is love'! Alas, it rules itself out as *the* Epistle by two related features which are *anathema* for today; namely, the spiritual smugness of 1 John 4:1–6 and a totally negative approach to the unbelieving world outside the Church and to 'the things in the world' (e.g. 1 John 2:15–17).

A heresy issue in an Epistle, we would say, does not automatically tell against it 'for today': it is often, as in 1 John, a real point of startled recognition of relevance for today's reader. Colossians, however, steeped in a local heresy issue (some would say now a pluralistic-environment problem), has no hope of being *the* Epistle for today because of the way in which it *counters* the heresy. Its major and recurring argument is assertion of the pre-existence of Christ and his agency in creation: an idea which, however profoundly true, passes popular comprehension completely today – and which even divinity students can hardly be persuaded to have the patience to *try* to comprehend! A pity about this strong contra-indication in Colossians, for within its small compass it handles remarkably well and comprehensively many live topics of today.

What about the Corinthian letters? Wonderful Epistles they are. Abundant in illustrations of Christian casuistry, they are also rich in theology. The doctrinal matter in, for example, 1 Corinthians 11, 12, 13 and 15 and 2 Corinthians 4, 5 and 6 is, at least, front-rank timely theology today or any day. (For today's burgeoning charismatic movement 1 Corinthians has, no doubt, high claim to be *the* Epistle.) But we have to judge the letters in their entirety. These letters are too big, we would say, their subject-matter too diffuse and their mood too violently variable for them to make impact upon us as *wholes* at all; still less for them to stand out as the *pre-eminent* unit (or units) among today's Epistles.

Four Epistles remain – Hebrews, 1 Peter, Romans and Ephesians.

Hebrews on the short list may seem strange. At a first reading, Hebrews is the most off-putting of all twenty-one Epistles. It is full of arguments based on Old Testament passages – arguments unconvincing to the modern mind. It is greatly, and detailedly, concerned with sacrificial ritual – a realm which most people today have antipathy to entering. New readers of Hebrews, we freely admit, are today likely soon to be non-readers. If only antipathies can be overcome and perseverance mustered, however, there will certainly be readers ready to say, having really 'got inside' Hebrews, 'For me this is one of *the* Epistles for today; maybe even *the* Epistle.' Why?

Not only is its Christology beautifully balanced. Its picture of the humanity of Jesus, completely real, tested and victorious in our human battle, is unequalled in any other Epistle and finds a thankful welcome in our day. So, too, does the allied element of atonement by 'sympathy'. For many today, also, prayer is made not only more real but real for the first time through Hebrews' teaching on the continuing intercession of the exalted, tested, human Jesus. Hebrews' distinctive presentation of the Christian hope – as an 'upward call' that carries demand and power for *this* life as well as summons to an assured goal beyond – is, more than many others, in tune with today's 'theologies of hope'. Where better than in Hebrews, too, is our contemporary sense of the Church having to keep moving – 'on the march' and refusing to be fossilized and anachronized by tradition, establishment and institutionalism – expounded and justified? In its brilliant chapters 11–13, on 'faith' and the on-going, outgoing pilgrim people of God, it meets both elements in 'for today' at one stroke, for as many in the Church still *need* to hear these things as the many who today *want* to. Again, far from institutionally minded though Hebrews is, no Epistle gives higher place to worship or sets more explicit store by Christians' assembling together (Heb. 10:25). This instructive balance is a most valuable corrective word for today. Finally, Hebrews glories in setting forth the uniqueness of Jesus Christ and the finality of the Christian revelation. Is not this very note missing and in special need of being heard and sounded again in our time? Many modern men, Christian ministers and missionaries among them, do not want it sounded: it resounds, they say, with a Christian arrogance, dogmatism and exclusivism they deplore. (Rightly, if it is there to be deplored!) Wanted or not, it is needed, for it is the Gospel. Acts, John, Paul and Hebrews are at one in this. Hebrews affirms it not only at greatest length but in best form for today, its opening verses (1:1–4) giving the best key for sympathetic – unarrogant – positive evaluation of all pre-Christian and extra-Christian revelation of God.

By its many-sided splendour and by its rich relevance for today, Hebrews surely justifies its place in the last four. Yet we recall the 'snags' of the initial barriers, uniquely high. These make Hebrews, we are bound to conclude, incredible as *the* Epistle for today, except for the few who have the commando courage and pertinacity to scale these heights. And even they may hesitate to say '*the* Epistle', when they realize that, despite all its strikingly timely things, Hebrews strangely never speaks explicitly of the *love* of God (or

Christ), that motif which is probably the most universally characteristic of both *need* and *want* 'for today'.

The first Epistle of Peter, like Hebrews, is a surprise 'semi-finalist'. Holiness, for instance, is a notion much out of contemporary favour. Not with Peter. His addressees are 'those who are travelling on the road to holiness' (1 Peter 1:2, Barclay). This obligation to be holy is stressed again as soon as verses 15–16; after only a brief gap the stress on their holy 'difference' comes back in 2:5 and 2:9. Coupled with the glowing verses in 1:3–5, affirming the readers' assured hope in the life to come, the Petrine holiness emphasis seems to call for and commend a brand of Christianity – one of pietistic 'superior' otherness and otherworldliness – held today to be obnoxious and benighted. We recall, too, some extremely weird 1 Peter ideas – Christ preaching to the disobedient antediluvians (3:19–20) and the ark as symbol of baptism (3:21–2). (Our rapport with the Epistles, earlier spoken of, is severely strained at such points.) And the teaching on women (3:1–6) will get no hearing from Women's Lib.!

The first Epistle of Peter, none the less, like Hebrews, can justify high 'seeding' for today. The serious reader (and re-reader) notes gratefully many emphases of our time; for example the *respect* for unbelievers (3:15, NEB) for whom we are to be ever ready to have an answer, the primacy given to persevering, constant and consistent, *love* (e.g. 1:22) in relationships, the call to witness primarily by a good and attractive life, even 'without a word' (3:1). Peter's doctrine of Christian 'difference', too, when understood and given justice, does not at all inculcate spiritual arrogance; on the contrary, it is wholesomely humbling! It reminds us of who we really are and whose we are in order to lay squarely upon us our responsibility to exhibit nothing less than the best in character and conduct. A reminder based on truth – and surely a need for today – and one that can only stir in us shame, humility, desire for amendment, as we reflect on how we fail to measure up: never arrogance!

Again, the freedom issue, so contemporary, is nowhere more neatly put than in 1 Peter: 'You must live like free men, but not like men who use their freedom as a pretext for vice. So far from that, you must use your freedom to become God's slaves' (2:16, Barclay). Perhaps the outstanding argument for 1 Peter as, at the least, one of *the* Epistles for today is the unrivalled attention it focuses on Jesus as the Suffering Servant and on the truth that, 'in his steps', his faithful servants in the world are going to be *suffering* servants! Our age, which has been so receptive to Jesus as Servant – and which has in consequence taken service so much to heart as the nub of the Christian's role – has, we suggest, largely ignored the *suffering* aspect of the service of our Exemplar. (Or we have made an over-facile assumption that 'service of the suffering' equals, or exhausts, 'suffering service'.) The first Epistle of Peter, better than any other Epistle, speaks to both our want and our need in this area: confirming on highest grounds that service – all service – is our business, and challenging us to accept, as is our need, that loyal discipleship today (while never masochistically *looking* for trouble) must expect, and cannot run away from, the experience of the Suffering Servant himself, of being 'despised and rejected of men'.

The first Epistle of Peter is not, however, *the* Epistle for today. When all has been said for it, it remains – doubtless because of its persecution setting – one of the most inward-looking and heavenward-looking of the Epistles. It is not aloofly 'holy', but it offers Christians a programme in and for the world that is one of little more than virtuous passivity. All that was possible in the circumstances addressed, perhaps; certainly not enough for today!

Romans and Ephesians alone remain to be considered. It could probably be foreseen that these two should be 'in at the last': they share favouring features unshared by the others.

Whether initially (in the case of Ephesians) or soon after first publication (in the case of Romans), both were early used as *circular* letters. Their contents and character fit them well to be encyclicals. They are of worthy length and weight; carefully planned; sustaining argument from start to finish. While they show a keen sense of involvement in the life-problems of Christian people of their day – *any*where, but also specifically in the particular churches where they are to be read – they are free of many of the particularities of more clearly 'local congregation-directed' Epistles (e.g. Thessalonians): particularities which later readers such as ourselves, in vastly different places and circumstances, may find irritatingly irrelevant. In short, more than any others, Romans and Ephesians are free of features which might tie their usefulness to some past situation and locality. They have thereby a head start on the rest towards being *the* Epistle for today: *any* today. It is still more to the point, however, to say that they owe this head start to their *positive* qualities – to the sheer pre-eminence in 'class' they show over all the others.

It is a pre-eminence which has been perennially acclaimed. We recall (largely with the aid of A. M. Hunter's *Romans*[4] and his *Introducing the New Testament*[5]) some tributes paid to these letters.

ROMANS

To Luther, Romans was 'the chief book of the New Testament and the purest Gospel'. In and since Luther's time, Romans is credited with having sparked off in century after century major movements of Christian revival and reform. Calvin said: 'If a man has reached a true understanding of Romans, he has a door of approach opened for him to the rarest treasures of scripture.' Coleridge's verdict – 'the most profound work in existence'; John Knox's (of Union Seminary, New York) – 'the most important theological book ever written'. Its phenomenal force is illuminated and explained particularly well by Brunner: 'There is no document of man's spiritual history in which passionate feeling, powerful thinking and inexorable willing are so mingled and combined as in this letter.'

EPHESIANS

John Mackay (Princeton) wrote: 'To this Epistle' – Ephesians – 'I owe my life', and Calvin was not prevented by his accolade to Romans from pronouncing Ephesians his *favourite* Epistle. More than once in this century it has been called 'the most contemporary book of the New Testament'. In 1930 E. F. Scott wrote of it: 'In some respects the most modern of all the New Testament writings.' He continued: 'We can feel when we look below the surface that the author is occupied with our own questions . . . and has answers to give . . . of the highest value.' W. Zöllner[6] expresses himself thus: 'At a particular juncture of time in the sixteenth century, the Epistle to the Romans was rediscovered; now we are rediscovering the Epistle of the Ephesians as a letter speaking to the Church.'

It is notable that in these quotations outstanding life-saving profundity is ascribed to both Epistles, though more often and explicitly to Romans, perhaps, than to Ephesians; attractive power and appeal, modernity and 'contemporaneity' (especially in our century) much more exclusively to Ephesians. This could be the mere chance outcome of random selection of quotations – yet there are powerful other considerations to support what this 'chance' suggests about Ephesians *for today*.

First: Ephesians, more than any other scripture, has in our time stimulated, and continues to sustain, the ecumenical movement. 'The doctrine of Christ and the Church is the central ecumenical issue of the mid-twentieth century; and

no document of the New Testament speaks more relevantly'
than Ephesians 'to this theme'.[7]

Second: American Presbyterians in the 1960s, taking on
the daunting task of formulating a new Confession of Faith –
to match the needs of our times – set forth the work of Christ
not in Romans terms (i.e. of justification) but in those which
are dominant[8] in Ephesians (i.e. those of reconciliation of
man with man in Christ).

This, it seems to us, is an absolutely sound, true reading of
modern man in relation to the dominant soteriological
terminologies of these rivals for the title of *the* Epistle for
today. Take modern man and *sin*, for example. He finds in
Romans that sin is law-breaking; that, whether it is Mosaic
law or law of conscience, it is *God's* law that is broken and
every man has broken it. Every man is a sinner who has out-
raged God and lies under God's condemnation. This picture
of sin in legal terms is likely to bewilder today's man outside
(and even inside) the Church: it is as likely to irritate.
(There is something so imposed and arbitrary about this
'law'; and this 'sin' is made such an individualistic affair!)
Modern man may well be at fault in this – not Romans –
but that does not alter the fact that *at this point of
time* Romans does but rarely 'get through' to him about
sin.

Modern man, though, knows what is meant by, say,
'things gone wrong'. He recognizes this condition all around
him (and even within him) as strife, war, division, apartheid
of any sort, disharmony, discrimination, alienation of class
from class, nation from nation, man from man. Very readily
he identifies such fragmentation at every level as *the* curse of
life. He knows himself as its victim; he recognizes his involvement in it and will own his share in creating it. He desperately longs for the key to the righting of the wrongness of it
all, to the lifting of the curse; to a life, a society, a world at
rest – and at one. Such a man, and he *is* today's man, is ripe
for the gospel of Ephesians! In that letter the whole 'plan of

H

salvation' is sct out precisely in terms of what God has done about 'things gone wrong', about 'sin' *so understood*, what he has as his assured final purpose to do for the whole fragmented world, and what place and work the Church has in this tremendous plan.[9]

A. M. Hunter's Dodd-based summary of Ephesians will recall for us its essential substance.

The Eternal Purpose

A divine intention runs through history. The ultimate reality is a Father, he has a purpose of love for all, and he wills community. But the cosmos reveals a 'great rift' – demonic powers marring the divine order, and sinful men at enmity with one another. Of himself, man cannot repair the rift; only God can, and God purposes to subdue all opposing powers – human and superhuman – to his will, and to create a great unity.

The Centrality of Christ

The Gospel is the good news of God's unveiled secret. This unveiled secret is Christ, who is not merely the Messiah of the Jews but the clue to history and the meaning of the universe. God's purpose is embodied in Christ's person and in the victory which he wrought by his dying, rising and ascending, and that purpose is the reconciliation of all created things.

The Glory of the Church

The purpose of God is to be realized through the Church. The Church is the Body of Christ, the social instrument which is to execute God's purpose in the world. The eternal God wills fellowship; in that fellowship Jews and Gentiles are now included; and this process will go on till all are reconciled to God in 'the Christ that is to be'.

In Ephesians there is, naturally, a wide range of precious ancillary matter at which the summary cannot hint. In the letter's complete course all the notes we hazarded to be needed and wanted in the Epistle for today are sounded. There is the note of love. There is the note of hope (not only for the individual and the Church but for the world – which makes it an extremely up-to-date form of Christian hope). There is a strongly *positive* church attitude to the world (an outward-going and in-bringing attitude), along with un-compromising insistence on the Church's true Christian 'difference': insistence too on its maintenance (through the ministry, sacraments, fellowship and prayer and 'the whole armour of God') of its spiritual power to *be* the Church and live a Christlike life. Not only the 'glory' or splendour of the Church is a needed theme given major place, as we have seen, but also the uniqueness and finality of Christ. Pro-minent on the list of Ephesians' notes, too, which are dis-tinctively contemporary as both want and need is surely its exposition of the purposefulness of history and of the mean-ing which, through our church membership, our individual life may find – and the contribution it may make – in relation to the sublimely great cosmic plan of God.

What of rival Romans? It does it no injustice that we for-bear to outline its (massive) contents or extol its multitude of virtues. The letter, unlike Ephesians, is so well known that it needs no rehearsing![10] Its magnificence is in no dispute. It merits all the praise lavished upon it in the quotations cited. It is gladly affirmed, too, that if we did 'go through' Romans (as through Ephesians) we could say it scored as highly in all, or almost all, the points of contemporaneity observed above in Ephesians. (Ample proof would be simply to go over our last paragraph, point by point, with Romans in mind.)

The one really decisive count in favour of Ephesians over

against Romans as *the* Epistle for today is the one explored above – the preferable-for-today terminology of Ephesians in respect of sin and salvation. There is a slight weighting in Ephesians' favour, too, in its comparative brevity. Perhaps because of it, Ephesians is able to give us a *sharper* presentation than Romans gives of a universe in which a great and gracious plan has been operating since the beginning of time, is presently (excitingly and visibly) at work today, and is going ahead invincibly to assured fruition.

It would be misleading to close without some acknowledgement that Ephesians – like every other Epistle (Romans included) – is not altogether 'easy going' for the modern reader. Three particular stumbling-blocks to an immediate understanding and full appreciation of Ephesians we recognize. One is the letter's treatment as of first importance – indeed as conclusive evidence of God's effective purposiveness – of the fact of Jew and Gentile reunited, in the Christian community. An initially ignorant reader may wonder at the seemingly excessive 'fuss' over this fact and at the great theological weight given to it. All this reader needs – but he does need it – is basic knowledge (available to him through study of any New Testament background primer or any Ephesians commentary) of the radicality and bitterness of the Jew-Gentile 'Great Divide' in the ancient world. That acquired, he will at once grasp, with the author of Ephesians, that in Jew-Gentile division overcome there was a visible miracle! The inconceivable good had actually been actualized, in the one Christian community!

A second stumbling-block is the prominence in the letter of reference to 'demonic rulers and powers in the heavenly places', 'cosmic powers in this dark world', and allied phrases. This is not the everyday thought-world of the 1970s! And yet, *isn't* it? Tillich has made the 'demonic' popular in intellectually respectable circles. Today's people, open to believe life (and *live* life) governed by 'luck', 'fate', 'chance', are in fact acknowledging such 'powers'. Young people's fascination with demonology, Satanism, etc., today is everywhere reported. How far away are they from Ephesians' 'powers of the air' and suchlike? Once again we believe that here is no *insuperable* obstacle to entering into the riches of Ephesians. For many potential readers such as we have indicated it is by no means an altogether strange thought-world they are entering in Ephesians. The others of us, as before, need only background study[11] – but we do need it – to make us sufficiently *au fait*.

The last of these stumbling-blocks is simply (!) the letter's language and syntax. In the Authorized Version its first chapter especially must frighten many people off completely. Verses 3–23 appear, as they do in our Greek texts, as only *two* sentences. Verses 3–14 make *one* sentence! If – in the Authorized Version – the content were immediately lucid, the terms' meaning plain, the prepositional phrases unambiguous in their attachments and intentions, the sheer length of sentences would not be so bad. But none of these saving conditions obtains. Nowhere in the New Testament is the work of the modern translators, especially the modern *interpreter*-translator (as Professor Barclay openly is), more *needed* and *vindicated* than in this letter, above all this *chapter*. Professor Barclay makes no fewer than fifteen sentences of the Authorized Version's two, and within these fifteen sentences he refuses to rest until he has wrested (from the desperately difficult Greek) what is at least *one* plain intelligible understanding in English of what the writer wrote. What effort has been required, but what a transformation into intelligibility for today has been achieved, and what service rendered for modern man, in his translation! When we put Ephesians on the pedestal as *the* Epistle for today, it is with the strong proviso that we are referring to Barclay's Ephesians, not King James's!

Three 'contra-indications', then, to Ephesians' selection as *the* Epistle, but none is fatal to it. Three hurdles, but none is unsurmountable. All the reader needs is rudimentary reading-up in the spheres of difficulty – and why should we be diffident in requiring this of any man? Rudimentary reading, along with, of course, *interpretative translation*, as in the Barclay New Testament.

With that combination, it is our guess, he will have no more qualms than have we in saying of Ephesians: 'This is *the* Epistle for Today.'

Mark 10:13-16:
The Child as Model Recipient

Ernest Best

In this paper we propose to examine the significance of Mark 10:13–16 for Mark and the community to which he was writing. We assume that he wrote in Rome about the time of the fall of Jerusalem. We begin by enquiring after the position of the pericope in the Gospel; is this due to Mark or did it previously stand in some relation to 10:1–12 and/or 10:17–31? It is generally recognized today that 8:27 – 10:45 does not represent a historical journey of Jesus from Caesarea Philippi to Jericho but is a Marcan construction. It contains two major themes: Christology and discipleship. Clearly the former of these plays no explicit role in our pericope.

H. W. Kuhn[1] has recently argued that 10:1–45 goes back to an original complex of pre-Marcan material containing three pericopae relating to divorce, wealth and position, roughly verses 2–12, 17–31, 35–45, but within each pericope we must allow for some Marcan editing. He argues:[2]

(a) Cleared of their Marcan redaction, these three pericopae are similar in 'form', that is, apophthegms with dialogue – on each occasion extended to include special instruction for the disciples. The three pericopae thus belong to the same *Sitz im Leben*.

(b) Viewed from the angle of *Traditionsgeschichte* they are similar, for in each Jewish-Christian tradition can be clearly recognized and in the second and third we find the equation of 'following after Christ' with 'imitation of Christ', a contribution from Hellenistic Judaism.[3]

(c) They are similar in content, taking up questions of behaviour which were of importance for the life of the community.

(d) The use of the first incident (10:2–12) and in part the second (10:17–31), which do not fit clearly into Mark's purpose on the instruction of disciples, is caused by his desire to use the third (10:35–45), which is very relevant. In order to use it he had to employ the whole complex; to it he added verse 1, verses 13–16 and verses 32–4.

We need to examine these points separately:

(a) The form of 10:35–45 is not the same as that of 10:2–12 and 10:17–31; in each of the latter we find a distinct break (before verse 10 and verse 23) between public discussion and the private teaching of the disciples. Moreover, the present form of 10:17–31 is largely due to Mark; in particular he has emphasized the element of private instruction of the disciples by the addition of verses 24, 26f., 28–31;[4] while 10:11f. may have already been attached to 10:2–9 in the tradition of Mark's church, he has probably inserted verse 10, thus producing the reference to private instruction.[5] Thus in the pre-Marcan *Vorlage* these pericopae did not necessarily have the same form. We must however agree with Kuhn[6] that they were probably used in a teaching situation – but this means little since it is true of a large proportion of the material in the Gospels.

(b) Granted that Jewish-Christian tradition is to be found in these three pericopae, this again is not unique; it is found in many Marcan pericopae. All material which did not originate in the Hellenistic Christian Church passed through a Jewish-Christian stage, though this stage will have left varying degrees of impression on the material. It is moreover doubtful if the equation 'following after Christ'='imitation of Christ' is as clearly found in 10:17–31 and 10:35–45 as

Kuhn suggests; the former is really only present in 10:17-31 and the latter in 10:35-45.

(c) This again may be admitted, but it is true of many other pericopae, for example 3:1-5; 7:1-21; 9:38-40; 12:13-17. It is hardly surprising that in a section on discipleship (8:27-10:45) there should be an accumulation of passages which deal with the theme as it affects community problems; this affords no reason for concluding that these passages co-existed as a unit - where else would Mark have placed them in his Gospel?

(d) We must agree with Kuhn that 10:17-31 and, in particular, 10:2-12 relate less directly to the main theme of discipleship, linked in its emphasis to the passion of Jesus through the passion predictions, than does 10:35-45; this does not necessarily lead to the conclusion that Mark had to use the earlier two pericopae in order to be able to use 10:35-45. Where he has used existing complexes of pericopae or logia it is normally because he wanted the first part of the sequence that he has done so (cf. 8:34-8; 9:35-50).[7] Kuhn recognizes the existence of pre-Marcan collections in 2:1-28 and 4:1-34;[8] in each case it is the first pericope which carries the major emphasis.

We can go further than merely responding to Kuhn's arguments. There are positive reasons to suggest that he is incorrect:

(1) Why did Mark add 10:13-16 at the precise point at which it now appears? It evinces Mark's interest in the resemblance of believers to children or in their relationship to one another; it would have been more appropriate to place it close to 9:36f., 42, where these themes recur;[9] they are absent in 10:1-12 and 10:17-31.

(2) If Kuhn is correct, then Mark has introduced into an existing complex a major geographical change when at 10:32, 33 he makes the first reference to Jerusalem as the end of the journey which began at 8:27. There is no evid-

ence for Mark making such changes in the complexes [he used.

(3) 10:35–45 were not themselves a pre-Marcan unity and therefore could not have formed the basic unit which Kuhn assumes they were.[10] If however 10:41–5 alone was regarded as belonging to the pre-Marcan complex this would not contain an apophthegm and so the pattern of three similar pericopae which Kuhn suggested (see (a) above) would be destroyed.

More recently still Morton Smith has argued that 10:13–45, with the insertion after 10:34 of the section of Mark which he has discovered in a letter of Clement of Alexandria,[11] represents a baptismal section which would have been used as a lection at the baptism of catechumens. It is impossible here to discuss the wider implications of the acceptance of what Smith calls the 'longer text' of Mark or even to examine the arguments for its existence,[12] but if we proceed from the assumption that at some time it existed, we need to consider Smith's claim that 10:13–45 as a unit deals with baptism. Either this unit existed prior to Mark and without the Clementine addition, or prior to Mark and with it and he then omitted it, or it was added to canonical Mark by Mark or someone else after the canonical Gospel had been composed, or was in the canonical Mark and later omitted by Mark or someone else. Since at the moment we are only examining chapter 10 to see if there is a pre-Marcan complex in it, all we need to do is to examine the coherence of 10:13–45 in respect of baptism. The relevant part of Smith's argument runs as follows: 10:13–45 is the place in canonical Mark where baptismal material is to be expected; 10:13–16 states the general prerequisite of baptism (become as little children); 10:17–31 states specific requirements (monotheism, obedience to the commandments, renunciation of property) which correspond to the standard preliminary instruction for baptism; 10:32–4, the credal prophecy of the passion and resurrection, provides both the assurance and the explanation of the rite's efficacy.[13]

Smith has much in his favour when he argues that the logical place for a baptismal lection in Mark would be in chapter 10. The first section of the Gospel is directed to outsiders, but from 8:27 the teaching is esoteric. At 10:32 Jesus finally departs for Jerusalem and death; the catechumen must be ready to accompany him, and so, directly after 10:34, he is baptized. Yet the exact position of the baptism must be more problematical. In 10:38f., which according to Smith[14] refers to the participation of the initiate in the sacraments, baptism is still hypothetical and not yet an accomplished fact. Baptism would then follow 10:40 much more appropriately, or could come at any point up to the end of the chapter. Quite apart from the positioning of the baptism in this section, the acceptance of the section as baptismal requires further support from the total structure of Mark. The Gospel appears to have been written for the benefit of an existing Christian community, to correct their doctrine and reform the quality of their discipleship, and was not written for the instruction of initiates. But Mark may have taken up an existing baptismal lection and included it at this point, its baptismal nature being easily recognizable to all his community; this would only be so if the baptismal nature of the pre-Marcan material can be clearly demonstrated; as we proceed we shall see that this does not seem probable.

At this point we must lay aside the possible baptismal nature of 10:13-16, for it is the meaning of this text in its context that we are attempting to discover; when we return to it we shall see that for Mark it is not primarily baptismal in meaning.

In 10:17-31 Smith draws attention to the irrelevance of verse 18, with its affirmation that God alone is good, takes this to be a credal confession of monotheism, and argues from it that it is a deliberate development of the original story in order to place a confession of monotheism immediately prior to baptism. He demonstrates how such a confession has a place in Judaism, and how in particular Mark 10:18 came to be quickly used in this way in Christianity, but fails to give evidence for its place in early baptismal liturgies. He also argues that the Ten Commandments were used from an early stage in Christian baptism by instancing Didache 2:1–3. This section of the Didache ('The Two Ways') is one of the earliest portions; but it is only in the existing form of the Didache, which is probably second-century, that it is related to baptism (at 7:1), i.e. the association is post-Marcan; 'The Two Ways' is pre-Christian, and so is the use of the Ten Commandments independently of baptism either in 'The Two Ways' or apart from it; we cannot then draw conclusions for Mark's use of the Commandments as necessarily implying baptism. Finally Smith draws attention to the abandonment of goods demanded in this pericope; how he expects this to support his claim to a baptismal reference is unclear since he provides no evidence for the practice elsewhere in the early Church and indeed denies its existence outside the community for which Mark wrote or which produced the complex. It is, moreover, very peculiar that if an example is to be given for baptismal instruction there should be chosen that of a man who refuses to follow Jesus! Surely there were better precedents. We thus see no reason to assume that 10:17–31 would have been taken in a baptismal sense.

10:32–4 can certainly be described as credal, but there are two parallel credal statements, 8:31; 9:31; what function do these other two play? This raises the more general point: Smith nowhere considers in any depth the total purpose of Mark's Gospel. We could argue that the disciples function in it as believers; their difficulty in understanding Jesus' words and actions corresponds to the difficulty of believers in understanding their faith; from the beginning it is addressed to believers; the logical place for the initiation

of a new member would be at its commencement, where
Peter and the others do begin to follow Jesus. Taken this
way, the pattern of Acts is followed, in which instruction
follows rather than precedes baptism.[15] Returning now to
10:33f. itself; if a credal type statement is desired, that of
9:31 fills the requirement much better because of its brevity;
the details of the passion given in 10:33f. seem wholly unnecessary for confessional purposes. Thus again, in the
10:32-4 passage we can see nothing to support the baptismal
idea.

Finally Smith argues that 10:35-45 is the sermon, the post-
baptismal instruction.[16] Its burden for him is: 'Practise
humility, make yourselves useful in the Church, and give
what you can.' As we have already pointed out,[17] verses
35-40 and verses 41-5 were united by Mark. Only one of
them can then have belonged to the pre-Marcan complex.
There is a baptismal reference in verses 35-40, so for Smith
it would probably be better to retain it, though, as we have
shown, it does not suggest that the baptism has just taken
place. Finally we note that the main lesson of verses 41-5 is
already found in 9:33-7, which on Smith's view is pre-
baptismal; it cannot therefore have any special baptismal
reference.

We conclude that, apart from 10:38f. and what we may discover in verses 13-16, there is nothing in 10:13-45 which
necessitates us viewing it as a baptismal complex which
Mark took up and used, nor for that matter is there anything
which suggests that Mark himself saw it as baptismal in
meaning.

Isaksson[18] prefers to connect our pericope with the one that
precedes it, 10:1-12, and regards the two together as a
church marriage catechism.[19] He does not argue the case in
detail: he holds that Matthew 19:1-12 is not dependent on
Mark 10:1-12, and appears to imply that since both are

united to the pericope about children (Matt. 19:13–15 and Mark 10:13–16), this linkage must be both pre-Matthean and pre-Marcan. This conclusion does not necessarily follow. Supposing Matthew 19:1–12 to be independent of Mark 10:1–12, all Matthew may have done may be to have substituted his account of the divorce pericope for that in Mark. To establish his point Isaksson would need to show that Matthew 19:13–15 does not depend on Mark 10:13–16. This he has not done and it is doubtful if it could be established; Matthew does omit Mark 10:15, but he has already used a parallel at 18:3. It is, moreover, highly doubtful whether Matthew 19:1–12 is actually independent of Mark 10:1–12.[20]

The suggestion of Jeremias[21] has commanded more general support: 10:1–31 is a pre-Marcan complex (Jeremias does not of course hold that it was pre-Marcan in its present form) dealing with 'marriage, children, possessions', three subjects on which all disciples would need instruction.[22] Mark 10:1–12 is a church rule about marriage, 10:13–16 is a rule about baptism, and 10:17–23 (25) a rule about wealth. Whether 10:13–16 dealt with infant baptism both prior to and in Mark is yet to be determined, but if in the pre-Marcan material it related in some way to the reception of children,[23] then there does exist some consistency among the pericopae; all of them then deal with discipleship in relation to something external: marriage partner, children, possessions. When we recall the easy way in which the early Church united the sayings of Jesus into sequences without caring much for logical consistency, we ought not to be surprised to find these three pericopae together; there is an easy progression, even if it is not logical, from marriage to children to possessions. This progression is more clearly exhibited in the pre-Marcan stage of the tradition than in the Marcan. It is difficult to see why Mark should have put the three incidents together, for the changes he has made in the second[24] and third[25] decrease their coherence in comparison with their pre-Marcan forms. If he still saw some common element in them which led him to put them together, it is much more probable that someone prior to him should have done so.

We must now turn to the content of verses 13–16 and look for signs of Mark's hand. It is joined to the preceding pericope by a simple καί, a characteristic of Mark's style. The subject of the impersonal plural (another Marcan characteristic[26]) προσέφερον is not that of verses 10–12, but it was Mark who introduced the reference to the disciples in verse 10; so this provides no grounds for rejecting a pre-Marcan connection of verses 13–16 to verses 1–10. Some scholars[27] suggest that ἐκπορευομένου in verse 17 implies that Mark, who introduced the reference to the house in verse 10, envisages all of verses 13–16 as taking place in the house which Jesus then leaves at verse 17. On the other hand, a verb of motion in relation to Jesus when he is calling disciples is Marcan (1:16, 19; 2:14).[28] It is probably safer to conclude that Mark is making no attempt to depict verses 13–16 as situated in a house. There is nothing internal to the incident which would require such a locality. The children who are brought to Jesus are not then to be considered as the children of the house of verse 10. There are thus few signs of Mark's hand at the beginning and end of the pericope. The whole of it is indeed bare of superfluous detail.[29] Verse 16 depends on verse 13a and requires it as introductory; some word must have been used to describe the approach of parents or other adults with the children to Jesus and, though the impersonal form of προσέφερον may be Marcan, the verb itself[30] is not particularly so and probably belonged to the tradition. Verse 13b is also essential to the story, though the use of ἐπιτιμᾶν may be Marcan. It also contains a Marcan theme, the misunderstanding of the disciples, but since verse 14 depends on it, in this instance the theme must have been present in the tradition.[31]

If Mark's hand is only to be traced minimally in the introduction to the pericope and not at all in the conclusion, is it to be seen anywhere else in the pericope? Verse 15 almost certainly did not belong to the story in its earlier stages,[32] for:

(1) Verse 16 is a fitting conclusion to verse 14 and fully answers verse 13a, making the pericope into an apophthegm or pronouncement story whose climax is an action and not a saying of Jesus; confirmation that the pericope could exist without verse 15 and be a true unity is seen in Matthew's omission of verse 15 in his parallel (19:13-15).[33]

(2) Luke, on the other hand, omits verse 16 from his parallel (18:15-17), for it is no longer necessary once verse 15 is there.

(3) We find evidence for the existence of verse 15 as a detached logion; there is a variant in Matthew 18:3[34] and probably another in John 3:5.[35] Once verse 15 had been introduced into the pericope, it itself became the climax and verse 16 redundant, as Luke's omission of it shows; probably this process was assisted by the solemn character of verse 15 in its 'amen' form. As we shall see, its presence also transformed the meaning of the pericope. If verse 15, then, is an addition at some stage of the tradition,[36] there is nothing in the way in which it has been added which indicates clearly whether it was added by Mark or before him. The motive for the addition probably lay in the catchword 'children' and perhaps also in the reference to the kingdom of God, provided verse 14c is not Marcan.

If we go so far as to eliminate verse 15 from the original story, there is a great deal to be said for also eliminating verse 14c. Without it, we have a straightforward incident in which children are brought to Jesus for him to touch them and are repelled by the disciples who are themselves rebuked by Jesus; he then embraces, touches and blesses the children.[37] This, incidentally, is the way in which the story has usually been understood popularly. The addition of verse 14c, still more of verse 15, turns attention away from the action of Jesus, which is itself an example to disciples on how they should behave, into a theological statement about the nature of discipleship: being like children. In verse 14c it is possible to give τῶν τοιούτων either, (1) its classical meaning, 'the Kingdom belongs to those similar to children', in which case it means something the same as verse 15 and Jesus is not saying anything which justifies his words in verse 14ab or his action in verse 16; or (2) the meaning it sometimes has in Hellenistic Greek and in the New Testament[38] as an equivalent of τῶν τούτων, 'the Kingdom belongs to these children', i.e. to these particular children or children as a class;[39] this makes Jesus say that children may be members of the Kingdom. Whether or not this was a possible meaning in the pre-Marcan stage, it surely cannot be after verse 15 has been added, since clearly it does not refer to the membership of actual children in the Kingdom; moreover, where Mark elsewhere (4:33; 7:13; 9:37; 13:19) uses τοιοῦτος, he gives it its classical meaning. When we also observe that verse 14c is a typical Marcan γάρ clause,[40] the most probable solution is that he has written it. If verse 15 had first been inserted into verses 13–14ab, 16, then verse 14c is easily explicable as a clause making the connection firmer; by the addition, Mark has emphasized verse 15 rather than the original meaning of the pericope. It is indeed possible that Mark himself added both verse 15 and verse 14c.[41]

If, then, we eliminate both verse 14c and verse 15, we have a simple account: children are welcomed by Jesus. The ancient world, unlike our own world, did not idealize children;[42] they were ignored as an unimportant section of the community; this is what the disciples wish to do; but Jesus ignores no one; he has time even for children, and to show it he is ready to bless them. Given this interpretation, we can also see how the pericope came to be attached to the preceding in the oral tradition; it follows the latter just as children follow marriage and it answers the question of their relationship to the Church – a question which certainly agitated some Christian circles (1 Cor. 7:14), though it of course contains no direct reference to their baptism. Once, however, verse 14c and verse 15 have been added, the weight of the pericope lies with them and its meaning changes.

Those who hold that the pericope was used to explain or defend infant baptism in the early Church[43] will naturally see this as an extension of the use to indicate the relationship of children to the Church. For this baptismal view in relation to children Jeremias[44] adduces four grounds:

(1) The verse was interpreted early as referring to baptism in John 3:5,[45] and then from Justin (*Apologies*, 1.61.4) onwards.

(2) The use of κωλύειν indicates a baptismal formula in which at baptism an enquiry is made whether there are any hindrances to it.[46]

(3) The imposition of hands (v. 14) is part of the ritual of baptism.

(4) Luke's substitution of βρέφη for παιδία and various other peculiarities of the Lucan text.

We need only comment briefly on these points; they are adequately evaluated and refuted by G. R. Beasley-Murray.[47]

(1) There is no direct literary relationship between John 3:5 and Mark 10:15;[48] the former could therefore have gathered its baptismal connections entirely independently of Mark; it moreover differs so much from the Marcan form that the forces which shaped each must have been very different.

(2) κωλύειν is an inherent part of the original pericope; it would have been pointless without it; we cannot therefore easily assume that it was part of a formula; indeed, positive

evidence would be required to demonstrate that Mark's first readers would have seen it as part of a formula.

(3) The laying on of hands (v. 16) was again a necessary part of the original account as a sign of blessing[49] and need not convey any idea of the impartation of the Holy Spirit as in baptism. Paul never relates the laying on of hands to baptism; when Jesus was baptized he received the Spirit in another manner. It therefore needs to be proved that Mark intended a reference to the Spirit in verse 16.

(4) Luke's substitution of βρέφη (suggesting very young children) may only indicate his adoption of an alternative word which was a favourite with him.[50]

In addition to these counter-arguments, there are also positive reasons for rejecting the baptismal interpretation of the pericope:

(a) It would be like a fish out of water in Mark's context. Throughout 8:27–10:52 he is stressing the great claims of discipleship. In the immediate context he sets out these claims in respect of sex and wealth, taking up two of the strongest impulses turning men from discipleship; to set between them a pericope saying, 'Discipleship means the Christian brings his children to be baptized', would be, to say the least, incongruous. Even if such an action could lead to persecution, there is no suggestion in our passage that Mark has this in mind.

(b) We have seen that verse 15, and probably also verse 14c, are later additions to the original pericope and they have transformed its meaning and become its climax.[51] For Mark, attention is not being directed to the need to bring children but to the requirement to be like children in receiving the Kingdom. This is appropriate to the main drive of the Gospel at this point, namely discipleship.

For similar reasons to those for our rejection of the baptismal interpretation, we must reject the view of Reploh[52] that Mark is dealing in the pericope with a problem of his own church in respect of the membership of children; the incident may at one point in its transmission have been pointed in this way but in its present setting, and with the addition of verses 14c and 15, it relates to discipleship. Likewise we must exclude from the Marcan interpretation any idea of a response to Jesus by the children;[53] even in the earliest form of the pericope the children are brought to Jesus; they are too young to come to him; they have not yet become 'sons of the Law' and are not responsible. Thus if the original pericope depicted Jesus' attitude to children, this has almost disappeared through the additions made to it and the context with which it has been provided.

What then do verses 14c and 15 mean? How do they bring a clearer understanding of discipleship? The child is clearly the model (v. 14c). But of what?

We can begin by dismissing that interpretation which takes παιδίον as the direct object to δέξηται,[54] 'whoever receives the kingdom of God as he receives a child'; this makes the child the model of the Kingdom. Certainly it is a possible meaning grammatically and it can be argued that it accords with Jesus' reception of the children in verses 13f. and is similar in outlook to 9:37. It necessitates, however, that we understand verse 15 in a different way from its parallel in Matthew 18:3, where this interpretation is impossible; Matthew presumably did not read Mark 10:15 in this way or he would have retained it, since it would then have been no longer parallel to his 18:3; equally, John 3:5 does not reflect this interpretation of Mark 10:15. These facts suggest that in the original meaning of the saying the child was not the model of the Kingdom. Within the Marcan context verse 14c blends more easily with verse 15 on the assumption that the child is the model for reception, which is the generally accepted interpretation. Lastly, in the ancient world children were not esteemed and their reception would not be indicative of the honour and respect with which we would expect the Kingdom to be received.

Ambrozic appears to provide a variant to this interpretation. He takes the pre-Marcan meaning of verse 15 to relate to the child as one who needs instruction: whoever would be a 'follower of Jesus must admit that he is unwise in matters of the Kingdom, and that his only way into the Kingdom consists in his acceptance of its mystery'.[55] However, when he comes to discuss the verse in its Marcan context, he appears to shift ground and interprets it: 'Whoever does not joyfully subject himself to the hidden kingdom offered by a hidden Messiah, by accepting it as a free gift of God, will not be allowed to share in its present and future blessings.'[56] He justifies this by paralleling the argument in 10:32–45 to that in 9:33–7, and from the latter he deduces that Mark's child is the 'one who is the last of all and expected to subject himself to others'[57] – and the disciple must serve even children. This appears somewhat muddled. In so far as it parallels the child and the Kingdom, it is open to the objections we made in the preceding paragraph. Additionally, while 'service' may be a parallel thought in 9:33–7 and 10:32–45, we are not dealing here with 10:32–45 and there is no necessary reason to assume that the 'child' functions in a uniform way in Mark.

We are then forced to return to some form of the traditional solution which makes the child the model for reception:[58] The Kingdom is to be received as children receive. But how does a child receive? Commentators have written variously of the innocence, simplicity, ingenuousness, receptiveness of children. All such interpretations, apart from the last, tend to romanticize the child in a way foreign to the ancient world. Légasse[59] argues strongly that the condition of becoming a disciple is following Jesus in faith (Mark 1:15), but we must beware of giving too theological a connotation to faith when children are being spoken of.

A child trusts[60] adults; he has confidence in them; he receives from them what they offer. So the disciple is to trust God and receive the Kingdom. The Kingdom is not a place or a thing; it is God's active rule; the disciple has therefore to allow God to rule in his life. This is not something which is completed once and for all in the act of becoming a disciple, but something which takes place continuously; hence the appropriateness of our pericope to a context of discipleship.[61] In the second half of the verse the kingdom of God is used of the future eschatological Kingdom (this is the more normal Marcan usage[62]) into which the disciple enters; that it is the future meaning which is intended is seen from 9:47; 10:17, 21, 23, 25, 30. Thus both present and future aspects of the Kingdom appear in the one verse: receptiveness of the rule of God now ensures membership of the future Kingdom. This might appear to be a kind of prudential ethic, yet the way in which receptiveness is understood in parallel to the receptiveness of the child takes away from this conclusion.

While at the beginning we said that Christology does not bulk large in this pericope, we may draw one negative conclusion. Sometimes the pericope is used to argue that we should treat others, in particular children, as Jesus treats these children. This would yield an implicit *imitatio Christi* Christology. This understanding of the story, even if it was once present in it, has disappeared through the addition of verse 15. Jesus is not just on the same plane as the disciples; he provides the teaching and understanding through which they become disciples.

Some Greek Words with 'Hebrew' Meanings in the Epistles and Apocalypse

Matthew Black

In his recent commentary on the Book of Revelation[1] Charles Brütsch estimates that of some 100 words employed by the writer which are nowhere else to be found in the New Testament – a high proportion of his total vocabulary[2] – no less than two-thirds are to be found in the Septuagint (LXX). Like all such calculations, Brütsch's results require careful control: the vast majority of the words in question are also familiar, or at least attested, in classical or Hellenistic Greek.[3] Moreover, unlike the study which inspired the title of this essay[4] or similar recent studies,[5] not many of the words employed in the Apocalypse from the Old Testament seem to have any special theological significance. Nevertheless, Dr Brütsch's result is an interesting, if not an unexpected one.

More important for our purpose now, however, is the fact that in a few cases of words and expressions in the Epistles and Apocalypse a 'Hebrew' meaning appears to have imposed itself on a Greek word; and even if the result is theologically unimportant, full account requires to be taken of all such possible Semitisms in the translation and exegesis of a passage.[6]

The following notes fall into three main categories. Firstly, a number of cases are examined where a 'Hebraism' or 'Semitism' in the Epistles or Apocalypse has been claimed and which seem to me to be so questionable that the explanation may require to be rejected. Secondly, some cases are discussed where certainty may not be possible, but where Semitic influences cannot be excluded as explanations of a particular usage. Thirdly, I add some examples where we are on firmer ground, and where there seems little doubt that the locution is a Semitic and not a Greek one.

1. SOME PUTATIVE 'HEBRAISMS'

Bauer does not hesitate to give θάνατος the meaning 'lethal disease', 'pestilence', though the only passages cited in support are from the LXX (Job 27:15; Jer. 15:2). In fact the term regularly renders Hebrew *deber* in the sense of 'pestilence', 'plague', in the Pentateuch and historical books as well as in the Prophets (Exod. 9:3, 15; 2 Kgs 24:13, 15). This meaning is so well established in biblical Greek and is so evidently the meaning intended at Revelation 2:23; 6:8, and especially at 18:8, that it seems one of the most certain of 'Hebraisms' or 'Semitisms' in the Book.[7] Moreover, neither classical nor Hellenistic Greek knows of such a connotation for θάνατος. While *deber* never appears to mean 'death' in Hebrew, Aramaic *mota'* (as Charles points out[8]) also renders *deber*, although the more regular Aramaic/Syriac word for 'pestilence' is *mo(au)tana* (TB Yeb. 44b; Pesh. Exod. 9:3). This might appear a hundred-percent certain Semitism, were it not for two things: first, the regular translation of Hebrew *deber* by θάνατος suggests that the Greek word, like the Aramaic, could mean 'plague', *the* 'death' (cf. the Black Death). Secondly, in modern Greek θανατικό means 'disease', 'pestilence'.[9]

The use of ποιμαίνειν in the general sense of 'to rule' is a well-known Hebraism in the New Testament (cf. Rev. 7:17), even though it involves a very slight extension only of the metaphorical use of the verb in Greek.[10] A vastly different claim is made for this verb by Charles at Revelation 2:27;

12:5 and 19:15. At 2:27 it translates Hebrew *ra'ah* or *ra'a'*, 'to devastate', or 'to break in pieces', as if it were *ra'ah*, 'to shepherd', 'rule'. The parallels at Revelation 2:27 and 19:15 are συντρίβεται and πατάξῃ respectively. Charles argues that ποιμαίνειν ought to be given the secondary Hebrew meaning 'to devastate, etc.,' in these passages, and appears to be followed in this by Bauer.[11] There seems little doubt that ποιμαίνειν at Revelation 2:27 =LXX Psalm 2:9 is a *mistranslation* of the Hebrew word, taken over by the writer of the Apocalypse, but does this mean that the latter understood the word in the sense of 'devastate', or that he intended to convey this meaning to his readers?

Charles argued that the primary sense of πρωτότοκος, 'first-born', at Revelation 1:5 is eclipsed by the secondary denoting 'chief' or 'sovereign', a secondary meaning deriving from Hebrew *beḵor*: Christ is here '. . . the sovereign of the dead, the ruler of the living . . .'[12] R. B. Y. Scott supports Charles, including the passage in his section on 'Mistranslations'.[13] No one can deny the primacy implied by *beḵor*, but to suggest that this idea 'eclipses' the full theological sense of this classic Christological term is precarious argumentation; the term has a rich background as an epithet of the Messiah (as Charles points out in his note on this verse[14]); it has also a distinctive Christian use as applied to Christ as 'the first-born of the dead' both here and at Colossians 1:18. It can hardly be a 'mistranslation', and if it is a 'Hebraism', then it should be classified as a Hebrew term and concept with profound Christological meaning.[15]

2. POSSIBLE 'HEBRAISMS'

One of the most debated ἅπαξ εἰρημένα in the New Testament is the meaning of ἀπεκδυσάμενος at Colossians 2:15. The verb, which appears again at 3:9, and its related abstract noun ἀπέκδυσις (2:11), represent a compound formation so unusual that they may even be ἅπαξ εὑρημένα of this Epistle,[16] in which case foreign influences would be in no way surprising. At 3:9 the meaning, 'to discard completely'[17] the 'old man' (as one does a garment) (ἀπεκδυσάμενοι), seems guaranteed by its opposite in the same verse, 'to put on', 'don', the 'new man' (ἐνδυσάμενοι); and this use, together with an evidently similar meaning for the noun at 2:11, has led to the popular interpretation reproduced in the NEB: '. . . he discarded the cosmic powers and authorities like a garment . . .' The main alternative interpretation is that given in the RSV: 'He disarmed the principalities and powers . . .' This gives ἀπεκδυσάμενοι an active force[18] and a sense which is said to be a classical usage of ἀποδύω and ἐκδύω, that is, 'strip', hence (of enemies) 'strip of arms', 'spoliare'.[19] This is the meaning adopted by Bauer[20] and Oepke[21] (entwaffnen): it is not favoured by Lohmeyer who considers such a meaning to be unattested.[22]

It is true the peculiar Pauline compound is unattested elsewhere, but this is true of any meaning that may be given to it. The active is used in Homer (Iliad, 18:83) of 'stripping arms of the slain' and 2 Maccabees 8:27 has τὰ σκῦλα ἐκδύσαντες τῶν πολεμίων, so that the meaning 'despoil', spoliare is not so far removed from that of 'entwaffnen', if it is not exactly synonymous. What most favours such a meaning for Colossians 2:15 is its context, for the verse continues (in the RSV): 'He disarmed the principalities and powers and made a public example of them, triumphing over them in him.'

So far no one appears to have considered a further possibility. The use of ἀπ(εκ)δύω(ομαι) in Greek may not be attested in the sense of 'disarm', but the corresponding Semitic root ḥlṣ supplies in Aramaic the regular verb 'to spoil', 'disarm'. Hebrew ḥalaṣ means 'to strip' and the Targum can use Aramaic ḥalaṣ in this sense,[23] though this could represent Hebrew influence. Talmudic Aramaic certainly uses the verb in the sense of 'to take off (clothes)', for example M. Katan, 25a. It is in Syriac that the word comes regularly to mean 'disarm', 'despoil', and renders generally συλάω or σκυλεύω, for example Exodus 12:36, 'they despoiled (ḥal⁽ᵉ⁾ṣu) the Egyptians' (LXX, ἐσκύλευσαν). So also at Job 24:19 (συλῶσιν); Acts 19:37; Romans 2:22; 2 Corinthians 11:8; Colossians 2:8 (συλαγῶγων). The presence of θριαμβεύειν at verse 15, to lead the 'powers captive in triumphant procession', may have encouraged the choice of a word which conveyed the image of the conquered 'stripped of their arms'. Professor Barclay's translation comes very close to this putative 'Hebraic' nuance of the word: '. . . he stripped the demonic powers and authorities of their power, and made a public spectacle of them, as if they had been captives in a victor's triumphal procession.'

Romans 3:4 cites Psalm 51:6 (LXX) in which νικήσεις (LXX (Rahlfs), νικήσῃς) renders Hebrew zaḵah. The NEB has: '(Against thee, thee only, I have sinned) . . . so that thou mayest be proved right (tiṣdaḵ) in thy charge and just (tizkeh) in passing sentence.' The verb in this context, parallel to ṣaḏaḵ, has the legal connotation 'to be cleared, declared innocent, blameless', 'to be acquitted'. But the root in Aramaic, and especially in Syriac, provides the regular verb for 'to conquer' (νικᾶν). Talmudic examples are: B. Nidda 52b: 'Thereby he overcame (z⁽ᵉ⁾ḵa') the learned'; Ab. Sara 10b: 'everyone who defeats (zaḵē) the King'. Syriac examples may be found passim. The LXX translator of Psalm 51:6 has given this Aramaic meaning to the verb, no doubt because νικᾶν is a much stronger expression. The NEB gets the best of both meanings by translating Romans 3:4 as 'win the verdict'. At 1 Corinthians 15:54 it is again a distinctive LXX type of rendering of the Old Testament Isaiah 25:7 which Paul takes over:[24] the original laneṣaḥ meant 'for ever' (NEB: 'he will swallow up death for ever'). Hebrew neṣaḥ also means 'victory', and this is clearly the sense St Paul intends the quotation to bear.

The verb νικᾶν is a favourite expression in the Apocalypse (it occurs 15 times, as compared with 10 times elsewhere in the New Testament).[25] The usage is for the most part normal Greek, the verb being used either transitively or absolutely, for example 11:7; 2:7, 11, 17. In some passages the context is forensic and is not far removed from the meaning of the verb at Romans 3:4, for example 3:21: the victory is that of one who shares Christ's 'session' with God in heaven after the Judgement. Is this nuance also implicit at 2:11, 17 (the white stone of the acquitted[26]); 2:26 (the victorious (acquitted) Christian will rule the nations); 3:5, 12? The imagery in several of these passages is that of the final Assize and its sequel. Is νικᾶν, as used absolutely in Revelation, the author's equivalent of the Pauline δικαιοῦσθαι (δικαιοσύνη), the divine acquittal, the 'winning of the verdict'?

Abnormal 'Hebraic' usage has been claimed for the use of ἐνίκησεν at Revelation 5:5 by R. B. Y. Scott[27] and C. C. Torrey.[28] Hebrew/Aramaic zkh has also the sense, close to its legal meaning, of 'innocent' when charged, of 'worthy', 'able'; for example Torrey cites Targum Psalm 118:22: 'He was worthy to be appointed King'; compare Bek. 60a: 'The mother of R. Huna proved able (zᵉka') to bear a son.' At Revelation 5:5 it is argued that the meaning is '. . . behold, the Lion of the tribe of Judah . . . has proved worthy to open the scroll . . .' The verb is then parallel to ἐδύνατο at verse 3 and ἄξιος εὑρέθη at verse 4. Is it possible that νικᾶν had taken over most of the meanings of Aramaic zᵉka' in Jewish Greek? Perhaps Scott and Torrey are finding problems where none exist: the RSV translates: '. . . the Lion of the tribe of Judah . . . has conquered, so that he can open the scroll . . .'[29]

3. MORE CERTAIN 'HEBRAISMS'

The claims that the specially Lucan use of (ἐν) αὐτῇ τῇ ὥρᾳ is an 'Aramaism' or 'Syriacism'[30] may be held to be weakened by the two Papyrus examples cited by Moulton and Milligan, for example P. Tebt II. 411[4] (ii/A.D.): '(on receiving my letter) come up instantly (αὐτῇ ὥρᾳ ἀνέλθε).' Nevertheless, whereas the expression seems to be rare in the Papyri (and in the Koine generally), it is the regular one in Aramaic or Syriac, for example bah bᵉšaʻta', literally 'in it, the hour', i.e. *instanter*.[31]

A related adverb to which less attention appears to have been paid by grammarians and lexicographers,[32] and for which no precise parallel appears as yet to have been forthcoming from the Papyri, is the LXX expression ὥραν μιάν at Daniel 4:19 for Aramaic kᵉšaʻa ḥaḏa, Theod. ὥσει ὥραν μιάν. The expression is idiomatic Aramaic/Syriac in the sense 'for a moment':[33] the NEB renders Daniel 4:19 by 'Daniel . . . was dumb-founded *for a moment*' (italics mine). The Syriac expression bᵉšaʻta' ḥaḏa renders Hebrew regaʻ 'eḥaḏ 'in a moment' at Exodus 33:5. Delling has drawn attention to the expression in the Testament of Job 7:12: ἐν . . . μιᾷ . . . ὥρα,[34] and to three similar expressions in Josephus which seem to reflect the same Aramaic idiom, namely, B. J. 3:228; 5:490, ἐπὶ μιᾶς ὥρας, and 2:457, 561, ὑπὸ μίαν ὥραν. The Josephan expressions are much better Greek than the literal rendering at LXX Daniel 4:16 (and in the examples given below for the Apocalypse): similar Greek forms of the phrase, but with the same meaning and all using ὥρα, occur at John 5:33; 2 Corinthians 7:8; Galatians 2:5, πρὸς ὥραν, compare 1 Thessalonians 2:17, πρὸς καιρὸν ὥρας.

The expression, usually μιᾷ ὥρᾳ,[35] is a favourite one in the Apocalypse, where English versions usually render literally by 'in a single hour'. 'In a moment' is an appropriate

English equivalent idiom for Revelation 18:10: 'in a moment [or even English "in a flash"] your doom has come'. So also 18:17, 'in a moment such great wealth has been destroyed'.

The same idiom may underlie the Mark 14:37 parallel, which should then be rendered 'Could you not keep awake for one moment?'[36]

In the LXX, ἀδικεῖν translates a wide range of Hebrew verbs, among which, however, 'ašaḳ occurs most frequently and is usually rendered in the AV by 'oppress'. Since one of the commonest forms of 'oppression', 'the doing of a wrong' to a person, is extortion or fraudulent dealing, LXX ἀδικεῖν='ašaḳ comes to mean 'to defraud', 'to cheat', for example Hosea 12:8 (NEB).

'False scales are in merchants' hands and they love to cheat' ('ašaḳ). The Hebrew verb takes an accusative of the person who is 'oppressed', 'cheated', and of the thing in which he is defrauded, for example Leviticus 19:13 (LXX), οὐκ ἀδικήσεις τὸν πλησιόν, AV 'Thou shalt not defraud thy neighbour' (NEB 'oppress'); Deuteronomy 24:14, οὐκ ἀπεκδικήσεις (v. l. ἀδικήσεις) μισθὸν πένητος, 'You shall not cheat with regard to the poor man's wage': a variant reading is Vulgate fraudabis, i.e. 'fraudulently withhold'. Compare T. B. Sukk. 29b, 'ošᵉḳē šᵉḳar šaḳir, 'those who withhold the hired man's wage' ('ašiḳ is used in the Talmud for anything that is outrageously dear).

This seems to be the meaning required at Matthew 20:13: the RSV has 'Friend, I am doing you no wrong', but 'I am not cheating, defrauding you', is the sense required by the context. The context at 1 Corinthians 6:7 strongly suggests a similar meaning: here the verb appears in the active and passive along with ἀποστερεῖν ('withhold'): 'defraud and rob' rather than 'injure and rob' (as in the NEB).[37] The more general sense of 'to wrong' seems more appropriate at 2 Corinthians 7:2, but the context again indicates that it is the wrong done by taking undue advantage of others

which is in the writer's mind (cf. ἐπλεονεκτήσαμεν).
Philemon 18 may be in the same category: the wrong
Onesimus had done his master was probably embezzlement,
by defrauding or cheating by theft or otherwise: NEB (my
italics) '... if he has done you any wrong [cheated, defrauded
you?] or *is in your debt*'. At 2 Peter 2:13 the original reading
is undoubtedly ἀδικούμενοι[38] (v. l. κομιούμενοι) and the
meaning similar to that at 1 Corinthians 6:7: we should
render 'being cheated of the reward of their wickedness':
Schrenk[39] renders 'wronged by the reward which is paid for
wrong-doing', which is not quite clear. The variant reading
'obtaining (κομιούμενοι) the reward of their wickedness' –
a completely different sense – is clearly an attempt to deal
with the difficult construction where a passive verb
(ἀδικούμενοι) is followed by an accusative: as a 'Hebraic'
construction there is no difficulty, the accusative may be
treated as an internal accusative, 'being wronged (=cheated)
with regard to (i.e. out of) the reward of their wickedness'.
The construction is partly due to the author's desire to
produce a play on words: we may compare Colossians 3:25.[40]
   While ἀδικεῖν is not an uncommon New Testament verb, its twenty-five occurrences include ten from
Revelation. According to Charles the verb in Revelation is
always used in the sense of 'hurt', except at 22:11 where
it means 'to act unjustly', 'to sin'.[41] A study of the nine
passages raises the question whether, in fact, the sense of
'hurt' or 'harm' (of impersonal objects) does full justice
to the writer's usage of this biblical Greek verb.
   Revelation 6:6 has given commentators and translators
special difficulty. The Black Horseman of the Apocalypse is
Famine. A voice cries out at verse 6 (NEB): 'A whole day's
wage for a quart of flour, a whole day's wage for three
quarts of barley-meal!' This is generally understood to
mean that the voice 'fixes a maximum price for the main
food-stuffs'[42] – a whole day's wage for the average daily

consumption of the workman. 'The proclamation, then, forbids famine prices, ensuring to the labourer a sufficiency of bread, and warning the world against such a rise in the price of cereals as would deprive men of the necessaries of life.' But how are we to understand καὶ τὸ ἔλαιον καὶ τὸν οἶνον μὴ ἀδικήσῃς? The RSV writes: '. . . but do not harm oil and wine!' The NEB renders: 'But spare the olive and the vine', where the words for 'oil' and 'wine' are taken to refer to the trees and vineyards.

Is it possible that ἀδικεῖν here reflects one of the uses of Hebrew 'ašaḵ, namely 'to withhold (fraudulently) what is due to or belongs to others'? The text of Revelation would mean: 'and do not (fraudulently) withhold the oil and the wine', with the possible intention of obtaining an exorbitant price.

In his commentary Swete points out that attempts to retain the etymological meaning of ἀδικεῖν have not been successful and concludes that 'in usage ἀδικεῖν, like our injure, has acquired a weaker sense, and is nearly a synonym of βλάπτειν'.[43] By way of illustration from biblical Greek, Swete drew attention to LXX Isaiah 10:20, where ἀδικεῖν is the equivalent of the Hebrew Hiphil verb hikkah (from naḵah), a verb with a by no means 'weaker sense', but, on the contrary, a very strong sense, usually rendered in English versions by 'smite'. Isaiah 10:20 is rendered by the NEB (italics mine): 'On that day the remnant of Israel . . . shall cease to lean on him *that proved their destroyer* . . .' The Testament of Simeon 5:4 uses ἀδικεῖν in a similar sense: '. . . your sons shall smite the sons of Levi with the sword (ἀδικήσουσιν ἐν ῥομφαίᾳ).' Certainly hikkah is generally rendered by such verbs as πατάσσειν, but ἀδικεῖν is evidently a possible rendering.

The Hebrew verb is idiomatically used of Jahweh 'smiting', i.e. sending judgement on the Egyptians with the plagues (Exod. 3:20, LXX), or 'smiting' the vines with blight (Ps. 104:33, LXX). Now this is precisely the meaning required in a number of the passages in Revelation which speak of the divine judgement 'harming' (=smiting, destroying) the earth, for example 7:2, 3; 9:4, 10. This force of the word is brought out by the NEB at 7:2, 3, where the four angels are given the power 'to ravage land and sea'. Generally, however, the English version renders, as the RSV here: 'to harm earth and sea'. The biblical Greek meaning is 'to smite, destroy (in judgement)'. A similar nuance may be required at Revelation 2:11, 'he who is victorious will not be stricken down by the second death'.

One of the best-known and best-attested Hebraisms in the Greek New Testament is the use of διδόναι=naṭan in the sense of 'to set, place':[44] thus Revelation 3:8 (NEB: 'I have set before you an open door'); 13:16 ('that they [indefinite plural?] should place a mark on their right hand'). Revelation 17:17 reproduces a well-known Hebrew expression with this idiomatic use, ὁ γὰρ θεὸς ἔδωκεν εἰς τὰς καρδίας αὐτῶν; NEB: '. . . God has put it into their heads . . .' Compare 2 Esdras 7:27 (=Ezra 7:27); 12:12 (=Neh. 2:12); 17:5 (=Neh. 7:5). Several other Hebraic uses of διδόναι have been noted. At 3:9 it is synonymous with and parallel to ποιεῖν, 'I will make certain of the synagogue', anticipating ἰδοὺ ποιήσω: 'Behold, I will make certain of the synagogue of Satan (who say they are Jews and are not, but are lying), lo! I will make them come and worship.'[45] At 2:23 it has the sense of 'requite' as at 3 Kingdoms 8:39; Jeremiah 17:10; compare Matthew 16:27 (ἀποδώσει).[46] At 20:13 ἔδωκεν means 'to give up, surrender' (NEB: 'The sea gave up its dead'), and Charles seems to be right in maintaining that this is not a classical or Hellenistic usage:[47] compare Judges 20:13, which has the more correct παρέδωκεν. A special feature of Revelation is its frequent use of ἐδόθη,[48] in particular with an impersonal singular, 'it was given (granted) to', and this again reflects the sense of naṭan meaning 'to allow, permit'; for example Esther 9:13, 'let it be permitted (δοθήτω) to the Jews'. So also at Revelation

6:4; 7:2; 9:5; 13:5, 7, 14, 15; 16:8.[49] Active 'to permit' is claimed for 2:7; 3:21.[50] Is 11:3 a similar case?[51] Revelation 8:3 speaks of 'offering' ($\delta\omega\sigma\epsilon\iota$) incense in respect of the prayers of all the saints, and this again is a LXX usage of $\delta\iota\delta\delta\nu\alpha\iota$ (e.g. Num. 18:12).[52]

Apollos the Alexandrian

A. M. Hunter

Now there arrived at Ephesus a Jew named Apollos, an Alexandrian by birth, an eloquent man, powerful in his use of the scriptures. He had been instructed in the way of the Lord and was full of spiritual fervour; and in his discourses he taught accurately the facts about Jesus, though he knew only John's baptism. He now began to speak boldly in the synagogue, where Priscilla and Aquila heard him; they took him in hand and expounded the new way to him in greater detail. Finding that he wished to go across to Achaia, the brotherhood gave him their support, and wrote to the congregation there to make him welcome. From the time of his arrival, he was very helpful to those who had by God's grace become believers; for he strenuously confuted the Jews, demonstrating publicly from the scriptures that the Messiah is Jesus (Acts 18:24–8, NEB).

A strange episode in Luke's record of 'the Road to Rome', as somebody has called the Acts! 'The case of the evangelist with the defective gospel' – so a modern journalist might describe this tale of the Alexandrian Christian who, on arriving in Ephesus after Paul had left for Antioch, learned the full truth of Christianity from Aquila and Priscilla, then crossed over to Corinth and proved himself more than a match in public debate for his Jewish adversaries.

Let us see if we can discover why Apollos, arguing the

same point with the Jews, was so much more successful than
Paul (Acts 18:5f.) and why in his preaching he drew after
him a band of partisans who cried: 'Apollos – not Peter, not
Paul – is the man for us!'

Question number one. What does Luke mean when he
says that Apollos 'had been instructed in the way of the
Lord'? (The Western text adds: 'in his own land', i.e.
Alexandria. If this is the right reading, the Gospel had
reached Alexandria, as it reached Rome, before AD 50.)
'The way of the Lord' (i.e. Christ) suggests the mode of life
taught by Jesus to his followers – the ethics of the Sermon on
the Mount. To this account of Jesus' moral teaching he
apparently added an outline of the main facts of Jesus'
earthly ministry.

Though some people today might reckon these adequate
qualifications for a preacher of the Gospel, Aquila and
Priscilla, quite rightly, did not. What gaps in his understanding of Christianity did they repair with such evident
success? How did they turn his defective gospel into an effective one (as witness what happened when Apollos went on
to Corinth)?

The first defect in Apollos was that 'he knew only John's
baptism'. That is, he had no proper understanding of
Christian baptism. In spite of Christ's great baptism on
Calvary, the Resurrection and the Pentecostal gift of the
Holy Spirit, Apollos had got no further in his understanding of baptism than those who had heard John on the banks
of Jordan. All he knew about was a water baptism which
symbolized a turning to God in penitence for past sin because
the day of the Lord was near at hand. Of Christ's great
baptism in blood (Mark 10:38; Luke 12:50) and of that
sacrament, deriving from it, in which men, baptized 'in the
name of Christ', were incorporated in the new community of
the crucified and risen Lord, so that they received forgiveness of their sins and the gift of the Holy Spirit, Apollos was
all unaware. Here Paul's friends Aquila and Priscilla could,

and surely did, enlighten his ignorance; and, though Acts does not tell us that Apollos submitted to Christian baptism, in view of Acts 19:1-7 we may be tolerably sure that he did.

Question number two. What further defect did Aquila and Priscilla discover in Apollos' conception of Christianity? Our clue to the answer is Acts 18:28. When, later, Apollos debated so effectively in public with the Jews, the burden of his argument was that 'the Messiah is Jesus'. Clearly, before his encounter with Aquila and Priscilla, the Christianity of Apollos had been (as Johannes Weiss puts it) 'Messianism without the belief that the Messiah had come'.[1] In other words, he had seen in Jesus the colleague and successor to John the Baptist, a prophet calling Israel to repent in view of the future coming of the kingdom of God. What Aquila and Priscilla taught Apollos was that *the Kingdom had come and Jesus was the Messiah*, that in fact 'the Kingdom is Christ himself'.

A momentous advance indeed! Near the end of his life Karl Barth, being asked if his concept of the person of Christ had changed over the years, made reply: 'Yes, at first I thought Jesus was the prophet of the Kingdom. Now I know he *is* the Kingdom.' This was the advance in his Christian thinking that Apollos owed to Aquila and Priscilla, and what a mighty difference it must have made to his preaching! For it is one thing to believe that Jesus is simply the prophet of the Kingdom, quite another to believe he is himself God amongst us in his saving sovereignty (which is what the kingdom of God means).

Here, since the scriptures were written for our instruction, let us add two comments not without relevance to our contemporary Christianity.

First, we have still in our churches many whose Christianity is as defective as was that of Apollos before he met Aquila and Priscilla. They are ready to see in Jesus a supreme prophet, a truly inspired man of God, the best indeed that has ever lived. But they boggle at the idea that he is

'God's presence and his very self' active in the affairs of men, God's saving purpose embodied in a man. But unless, as Paul, Priscilla and Aquila surely held, God was really *in* Christ, uniquely and decisively, we have no Good News for a sin-sick world. If Jesus is not the kingdom of God incarnate – God manifest in the flesh – but only one more man, however good and great and gifted, we had better erase the word 'Gospel' from our vocabulary. We are in no better case than the Unitarian preacher who came to win converts to his creed among the down-and-outs of Aberdeen. On the third night of his mission a fallen woman out of the crowd told him that he had better pack up and go home. 'Your rope', she explained, 'is not long enough for the likes of me.'

The only Christianity with a future before it is one which unequivocally proclaims that God once intervened decisively in human affairs in the person of his Son Jesus Christ, and holds that (as another Aberdonian said) 'the key to history is the historic Christ, above history and in command of it, and there is no other'.[2]

Our second comment is more practical. How wisely Aquila and Priscilla acted when they found how imperfect was Apollos' understanding of the faith! They might well have been tempted to stand up in the synagogue and publicly correct – or even denounce – his errors. Instead they took him in hand privately and taught him 'the truth as it is in Jesus'. And what spiritual dividends that private counselling yielded! Thanks to his two Christian mentors, Apollos now had a real gospel to preach, so that when he moved on to Corinth, he proved not only a highly gifted evangelist but, by virtue of his expertise in the scriptures, became (in T. W. Manson's phrase) 'the patron saint of the Christian evidence societies; the father of apologetics'.[3]

1. APOLLOS IN CORINTH

Now, using not only Acts 18:24-8 but 1 Corinthians 1-3, let us follow Apollos westwards to Corinth.

It was probably late in AD 52 that Apollos began his mission in that great pagan city. There not only did he debate with the Jews but he helped to water the young shoots of Paul's planting: 'I planted, Apollos watered,' said Paul (1 Cor. 3:6), 'but God gave the growth.'

Yet the mission of Apollos was to produce two very different effects.

(1) According to Acts 18:28, in public debate with the Jews he proved himself a redoubtable dialectician, proving from the scriptures that the Messiah was Jesus. The verb Luke uses to describe the success of his dialectic – *diakatelegchein* – is a very strong one. It means that he 'floored' his critics.

(2) The second result was not so happy. From 1 Corinthians 1-3 we gather that, *all undesignedly*, the preaching of Apollos sparked off that foolish party strife, reported by 'Chloe's people', which, among other things, moved Paul in AD 55 to write 1 Corinthians. Yet these two things – his success in debate with the Jews and the outbreak of party strife in the Corinthian church – may well not have been so unrelated as might at first appear.

To explain this, we must consider what manner of man Apollos was. 'I think', said 'Rabbi' Duncan,[4] 'that he was an intellectual – a man after the type of Philo the Jew.' This is a shrewd comment with probably a good deal of truth in it. Recall Apollos' *patris* and his origins. While Apollos had been growing up in the ghettoes of Alexandria, the leading theological thinker there was beyond any doubt Philo (20 BC – AD 50). What was Philo's particular line of theological expertise?

Convinced that the monotheistic God of the Jews was the

one God of the Greek philosophers, Philo pursued what he called 'the path of figurative interpretation [i.e. of the scriptures] so dear to philosophical souls'. So expert was he in the allegorical exegesis of the Old Testament that he was able to find in passage after passage of the Pentateuch the best wisdom of the Greeks – notably Platonism but also Stoicism. (Thus, to take two examples, he derived the three Greek cardinal virtues – prudence, courage, and self-control – from the three rivers – Pishon, Gihon and Tigris – mentioned in Genesis 2, and he held that it was the *Logos* (of Stoic thinking) which spoke to Moses in the burning bush.)

Whether Apollos had ever met or heard of Philo in Alexandria – and it is not impossible that he had – it is likely that he took the same theological line as his great co-religionist. Here we may find the explanation of why he succeeded in those public debates with the Jews of Corinth. Master of allegorical exegesis, he was able to find in the Old Testament type after type of Jesus the Messiah and his saving work.

On the other hand, when he preached, he knew well how to employ the wisdom of Hellas in the service of the Gospel. Such cultured preaching was well calculated to charm Greeks who were quick to contrast it with the less stylish preaching of Paul who kept hammering away at the cruciality of the Cross. Thus there arose that clique in the church at Corinth whose watchword was 'I am of Apollos', as doubtless it was in reaction to the Apollos faction that there originated the party of Paul, their first father in God (1 Cor. 4:15). When this happened, is it surprising that yet others said in effect, 'A plague on both your parties!' and lined themselves up under the banner of Peter, the leader among the original twelve apostles – more especially if (as seems probable) Peter had in fact visited the church at Corinth?

If we are right, then, the whole trouble originated in the excesses of the Apollos party. It was these which led Paul to say so many hard things about 'the wisdom of men' in

1 Corinthians 1–3. One point, however, must be underlined. Never once in his letter does Paul disparage Apollos himself. On the contrary, he regards him as a true colleague (1 Cor. 16:12), a fellow-agent with himself in the propagation of the Gospel (1 Cor. 3:5ff.): theirs, he says, had been good team-work for God. What grieved Paul was not his colleague Apollos but his supporters, those silly sciolists who so idolized the brilliant Alexandrian that they were wrecking the whole peace of the Church. Such adulatory advocacy of a church leader and his gifts, to the injury of the whole Church, is not without its parallels in the later story of the Church.

The gravamen of Paul's complaint against the Apollos faction was that they made of the Gospel a philosophy, a wisdom, a *gnosis*, when, properly understood, it was a spiritual *power* reaching down with God's redeeming grace in the crucified Christ to the very moral foundations of life. ('To be sure,' Paul says, 'I have a secret wisdom of my own, but it is for mature Christians, not babes in Christ, like you.' See 1 Corinthians 2:6ff. and 3:1ff. By this Paul probably meant the wider implications of God's redemption of the race in Christ – the divine plan for the world – as he sketched it out later in Ephesians.) For Paul, the Gospel was not a *gnosis* but a *dynamis* – God's *dynamis*, centred in the Cross, which brought 'righteousness and sanctification and redemption' (1 Cor. 1:30), that is, real forgiveness, a new life of holiness created in men by Christ, and deliverance from bondage to old evil ways. 'Jews demand signs,' he said, 'and Greeks seek wisdom, but we preach Christ crucified, a stumbling block to Jews and folly to Gentiles, but to those who are called, both Jews and Greeks, Christ the power of God and the wisdom of God' (1 Cor. 1:22f.).

Accordingly the sum of Paul's counsel to the quarrelling Corinthians is this: 'An end to all these factions, or you may have to answer to God for them! We apostles – Apollos, Peter and myself – are simply human agents in bringing you the Gospel. Ministers of Christ we are, fellow-labourers in the service of God, as you are God's field or building on which we work. Therefore never make mere men a cause for pride!'

But, as often happens in his letters, Paul rounds off his admonitions with a sentence which lifts us from the pettiness of the Corinthian party strife into the spiritual empyrean of God's great purpose in Christ: 'For all things are yours, whether Paul or Apollos or Cephas or the world or life or death or the present or the future, all are yours; and you are Christ's; and Christ is God's' (1 Cor. 3:21f.).

To a church bedevilled and rent by party strife what a salutary recall to the true range and greatness of the Gospel! Does it not speak to us also with our ecclesiastical party labels – 'I am of Knox', 'I am of Luther', 'I am of Wesley' – and our all too narrow and parochial concepts of what Christianity is?

'All things are yours', Paul tells us, as he did the Corinthians. The whole world-order – all men and times and circumstances – belongs to the Christian, and Christianity is a way to meet and master all that it holds. But how? What is the secret?

The answer is in the next four words: 'And you are Christ's.' When Paul says, 'You belong to Christ', this is not just a piece of pious blah. What he means is that the essential thing in Christianity is a personal relationship to Christ. So often we talk as if Christianity were simply a set of opinions about this or that current issue or problem – be it pacifism, pollution (physical and moral) or 'bishops in presbytery'. Of course on such matters the Christian is called to judge and decide. But the essential, the indispensable, thing in Christianity is a personal relationship to a living person, to Jesus Christ, the King and Head of the Church.

But having said this, Paul is not quite finished, for he clinches the whole matter with four further words: 'And Christ is God's.' Christ is not merely some people's private hero, or the personal property of any religious sect or party.

He is part of the last reality of the universe. The supreme truth about the Carpenter is that he comes from the Creator, from the Power 'which moves the sun and the other stars'. And when we build on Christ, we are building not on any shifting quicksand but on the eternal granite, which is God.

Thus even petty party strifes have their precious by-products if, as at Corinth, they can evoke such splendid statements of the grandeur of the Gospel.

2. APOLLOS AND HEBREWS

Now, at the end, let us come back to 'our brother Apollos' as Paul calls him (1 Cor. 16:12).

Some people may think that it is a profound pity that the New Testament canon does not include a letter – or a sermon – from Apollos: some sample of the way in which he so expounded the Old Testament as to make it foreshow Christ and his work, and harnessed the wisdom of Hellas in the service of the Gospel. With this in our hands, how much better might we have appraised the apostle whom Paul accounted a true fellow-labourer in Christ's service and a worthy successor to himself in the gospel 'field' at Corinth!

And yet, may not our regret at lack of a letter from Apollos be perhaps misplaced?

Whose hand penned the Epistle to the Hebrews, that religious masterpiece which portrays Christ as the perfect Priest who by his self-sacrifice on the Cross has opened up for us a new and living way into the presence of God; which contends that Christianity is the fulfilment of all that the ritual of the Jewish Law – the whole system of priest and sanctuary and sacrifice – could only foreshadow; which in passage after passage calls on its readers (probably in Rome) to go forth into the world with the Gospel under the leadership of the unchanging Christ?

It was not Paul's hand. On this modern scholars are agreed. Yet it is the work of a man belonging to Paul's circle (see Heb. 13:23). Why should it not have been Apollos, as Luther and many good modern scholars have surmised? Go back to Luke's description of Apollos in Acts 18 from which we started. There Luke tells us four things about Apollos:

(1) He was a Jewish Christian.
(2) He was an eloquent preacher.
(3) He was a native of Alexandria.
(4) He was a *maestro* with the scriptures.

All these things fit Apollos like a glove. Without doubt the nameless author of Hebrews was a Jewish Christian. His highly rhetorical style, plus his habit of stopping to exhort his readers, proclaim the gifted preacher. He interprets Christianity in terms of the two-storeyed view of reality - the shadowy and the real - as Alexandrians like Philo did (see especially Heb. 8:5; 9:23ff.; 10:1), which goes back to Plato. And he allegorizes the scriptures -- witness what he does with Melchizedek (Gen. 14:17f.) in chapter 7 - to show that Christ and his salvation are the fulfilment of the types and cultus of Judaism.

We cannot *prove* that Apollos wrote Hebrews. But if it was not the eloquent Alexandrian, it must have been, spiritually speaking, the twin-brother of the man with the defective gospel whom Aquila and Priscilla befriended in Ephesus, and to whom they taught the full truth about Christ and the kingdom of God.

Five Hard Sayings of Jesus
William Neil

PEACE THROUGH STRIFE

You must not think that I have come to bring peace to the
earth: I have not come to bring peace, but a sword (Matt.
10:34, NEB).

The birth of Christ which we celebrate at Christmas is
generally thought of as promising peace on earth (Luke
2:14), and in one of the great choruses of Handel's *Messiah*
Christians have always understood the words of Isaiah 9:6
about the coming of the 'Prince of peace' to refer to Jesus.
On the first Christmas of World War I German and British
troops in the front line spontaneously left off shelling each
other and joined in singing Christmas carols and making
gestures of goodwill, because they felt instinctively that war
in all its horror was the utter denial of the spirit of the Christ
whom both sides had been brought up to honour. Since then
in time of war a Christmas truce, official or unofficial, has
seemed to be the right way to recognize at least for this short
period that peace and not war is what Christianity stands
for. Did not Jesus say: 'All who take the sword die by the
sword' (Matt. 26:52, NEB)?

Yet here Jesus appears to be saying something quite
different, namely that his mission was not to bring peace to
the world but a sword, almost as if he were proclaiming a
holy war, as followers of Mohammed were to do several
centuries later. And indeed, taken out of their context these
words were used by fanatical Scottish Covenanters in the

religious wars of the seventeenth century to justify their blasphemous war-cry: 'Jesus and no quarter!' If, however, we look at the words that follow verse 34 Jesus' meaning becomes clear. Verses 35 and 36 (NEB) continue the thought of verse 34: 'I have come to set a man against his father, a daughter against her mother, a son's wife against her mother-in-law; and a man will find his enemies under his own roof.' These words are adapted from Micah 7:6 and they make it plain that Jesus is not speaking of war at all, either of war between nations or of civil war within the same nation, but of conflict within the same family. St Luke's version of the same saying (Luke 12:51, NEB) confirms this: 'Do you suppose I came to establish peace on earth? No indeed, I have come to bring division.'

We can see this happening in the story of the early Church when within ordinary families one or two members would become converts to Christianity as a result of the evangelism of the missionaries. Other members of the family would choose to continue in their old faith – whether Jewish or pagan – and argument, discord and bitterness ensued. The harmony of the family was destroyed. But we do not need to look back to the ancient world. Any missionary in the young churches overseas today can tell story after story of the breaking-up of families in India, Africa and elsewhere when some have responded to the Christian Gospel and others have preferred to continue in their old ways. The result is a divided house. It must require superhuman courage for a member of a Hindu or Moslem family to break with the traditions of centuries and face the contempt, and indeed hatred, of relatives who see conversion to Christianity as a betrayal and an unforgivable sin. Mahatma Gandhi, who had a deeper understanding of the Christian way than most nominal Christians in the Western world, could not bring himself to sever his connection finally with the Hindu background in which he had grown up.

There is, however, a wider sense in which Jesus' words in

Matthew 10:34 may be taken. Having lived through two major wars in half a century and with the ever-present shadow of possible annihilation darkening our future, most of us think of peace as the absence of armed conflict and in some moods can wish for nothing better for our children than that they should grow up in a world from which war and the fear of war has been banished for ever. But as Studdert Kennedy said, 'War is kinder than a Godless peace.' There are some kinds of peace that are not worth having – peace at any price, peace that perpetuates injustice, peace that exists under tyranny. Europe and the world could have had peace under Hitler's Thousand-year Reich, with concentration camps and gas chambers for those who ventured to criticize the regime.

Any country could secure industrial peace by giving in to the militants in the trade unions and by distributing the biggest slices of the national cake to those unions which are prepared to hold the country to ransom. It would no doubt mean galloping inflation and eventual national bankruptcy, but it would bring peace of a kind. By the same token, a right-wing dictatorship could also ensure industrial peace by repression and intimidation of the workers, by using the method of mass unemployment and by practising the techniques of the modern police state. This too would not be a peace worth having.

Christ certainly came to bring peace, as every page of the New Testament confirms, but he stood for real peace and not a bogus peace. His peace must be fought for, and that involves conflict and division, as his words in Matthew 10:34 remind us. As followers of Christ, we are committed to fight against the evil in ourselves and in our society in the light of the guidance we have been given. It is a battle against greed and selfishness, against cruelty and oppression, against injustice and indifference, wherever they may be found. The Gospel is a gospel of peace through strife, not peace through apathy or evasion of responsibility. Peace in the home, the office, the factory, and in society at large is not achieved by everyone agreeing with everyone else but by everyone standing up for what he believes to be true and right. Of course this will mean disagreement and discord, opposition and often bitterness. But the peace that Christ came to bring can only be realized by striving to reconcile our differences in charity but with honesty, or, as St Paul puts it, by speaking the truth in love (Eph. 4:15).

RECONCILIATION NOT RETALIATION

If someone slaps you on the right cheek, turn and offer him your left (Matt. 5:39, NEB).

Love your enemies (Matt. 5:44, NEB).

Jesus' words about 'turning the other cheek' are often quoted derisively by opponents of Christianity as the supreme example of the futility and impracticality of Christ's teaching. What would have happened, they ask, if we had turned the other cheek to Hitler? And are we to stand by benevolently while a thug attacks our mother, only murmuring that our sister will be back shortly? Questions of this sort are obviously based on muddled thinking or wilful misunderstanding. There is, of course, some excuse for misunderstanding if we confine ourselves to the Authorized Version: 'Resist not evil; but whosoever shall smite thee on thy right cheek, turn to him the other also.' This certainly sounds like a demand by Jesus for non-resistance in cases of violent attack.

The New English Bible, however, makes it plain that this is not so. Jesus is contrasting the Old Testament principle of 'an eye for an eye and a tooth for a tooth' (Exod. 21:23–5), the law of retaliation (Matt. 5:38), with the new principle by which his followers must be guided, the desire for reconciliation. 'Do not set yourself against the man who wrongs you', he says in verse 39, that is, do not retaliate in cases of unfriendly attacks upon ourselves. But putting up with a slap on the face is obviously not the same as risking a blow with a cosh from a burglar. In that case, self-defence would be common sense, and protection of helpless victims a Christian duty. A slap on the face is merely a picturesque way of describing a personal insult, and, in this event, turning the other cheek means refusing to return the insult but rather ignoring it. This saying has therefore nothing to do with arguments for or against pacifism, violence or non-violence, or indeed political, military or police action of any kind. Jesus is dealing purely with personal relationships.

And as so often in his teaching, he throws out a challenge by startling his listeners with the unexpected. They had become accustomed to his way of making people think by saying something amusing: 'If someone gives you a clout on the side of the head . . .' (pause while they cudgel their brains as to what they were supposed to do! – then comes the least likely answer) '. . . let him clout you on the other side as well!' We can see from the next few verses (Matt. 5:40–2) that Jesus does not mean his hearers to take him literally, for he goes on to talk of a man being sued in a law-court for the recovery of his 'shirt' (the long undergarment worn next to the skin which, together with the 'coat' on top for cold weather, formed the sum total of a man's clothing). If this happens, says Jesus, let your creditor have the coat as well, which would of course leave the man naked except for his loin-cloth!

The other two illustrations make it abundantly clear that Jesus' language is figurative. The first is that of a Roman legionary picking on a passer-by and ordering him to carry some heavy load for a mile along the road, as Simon of Cyrene was compelled to carry Jesus' cross (Mark 15:21). If this happens to you, says Jesus, offer to carry it twice as far – the proverbial 'second mile' – obviously the last thing a reluctant conscript would dream of doing. But it is the principle of responding to harshness with kindness that Jesus

B.S.   L is commending. So with Jesus' last example: 'Do not turn your back on a man who wants to borrow.' To obey this literally would encourage spongers, and reward the shiftless and thriftless at the expense of those who work for their living. Jesus is obviously not commending indiscriminate charity, which is demoralizing, but rather urging us to cultivate the spirit of generosity. While this has strictly nothing to do with avoiding retaliation, it does show that the whole passage is not concerned with laying down laws for Christian behaviour but with the attitude a Christian should adopt in dealing with people in general – reconciliation and magnanimity must point the way.

Jesus crystallizes his teaching on this aspect of the Christian life in the memorable words: 'Love your enemies' (Matt. 5:44). Like his previous saying about 'turning the other cheek', this has provided a happy hunting-ground for scoffers at the remoteness of Christian teaching from everyday life. Are we supposed to love IRA terrorists who spread death and destruction among innocent people? And are Christian Jews expected to feel a warmth of affection for Arab attackers, which ordinary Israelis are under no obligation to share? Let us once more see these words of Jesus in their proper context. He is still talking about personal relationships and not about nations at war or enemies of the state. More important, when he says 'love' he does not mean 'like'. How could we possibly be asked to 'like' someone who is bent on breaking up our home-life, destroying our marriage, leading our children into bad habits, spreading malicious gossip about us or making trouble for us in our jobs? Yet Jesus tells us we should 'love' such people. What does he mean?

Clearly he does not expect his followers to love those who do them an injury in the same way as they love their wives and families, their parents and their best friends. He urges us, however, to take God as our example, who sends the blessing of rain and sunshine on all alike, good and bad, honest and dishonest. We must show a like goodwill in our own circle to all and sundry, whether we like them or not, helping where our help is needed, in the spirit of the Good Samaritan. St Paul grasps the sense of our Lord's words when he says: 'Do not let evil conquer you, but use good to defeat evil' (Rom. 12:21, NEB). Disregard of personal insults, forgiveness of wrongs done to us, generosity of spirit to friends and enemies alike – these are the marks of Christian discipleship.

THE POWER OF FAITH

If you have faith no bigger even than a mustard-seed, you will say to this mountain, 'Move from here to there!', and it will move; nothing will prove impossible for you (Matt. 17:20, NEB).

Two elderly sisters who had spent all their lives in a Welsh mining village came home one Sunday from chapel, where they had heard a powerful sermon on the faith that can move mountains. At the back of their cottage there was an enormous slag heap which completely blocked their view and which was a constant irritation. One sister said to the other: 'If faith can move mountains, surely if we pray hard enough we can get rid of this horrible slag heap.' So they pulled down the blinds and prayed very hard that the offending blot on the landscape would disappear. When they pulled up the blinds again the monstrosity was still there. 'You see,' said the older sister, 'I knew all the time that it wouldn't move.'

We need not feel superior and think that they should have known better, for on the face of it they were doing exactly what Jesus had commanded. Nor should we point out that obviously one at least of the sisters had no faith at all that their prayers would make the slightest difference to the slag heap. But neither Jesus nor his audience thought for a moment that this saying had anything to do with literally moving tons of earth and stone. Whatever else Jesus was, he was a realist, who did not talk about things that only happen in fairy-tales as if they had anything to do with religion. But he was a master of picturesque illustration, who told people to take the planks out of their own eyes before they started looking for specks in the eyes of their neighbours, who talked of those who were prepared to gulp down a camel but were so fastidious that they would choke over swallowing a midge, or who, in speaking of God's care and concern for each of us, said that our heavenly Father had actually counted the hairs on each of our heads.

By describing things that are impossible or incredible in this way, Jesus arrested the attention of his Palestinian audience and made them think of the essential meaning behind his exaggeration and overstatement. So in this saying it would be quite clear to the listeners that Jesus was not really talking about mountains or, for that matter, about mustard-seeds, which were proverbially the smallest of all seeds. He was talking about *faith*, and impressing on the audience that even the tiniest particle of faith could achieve results that are comparable to shifting mountains. In Mark's Gospel (Mark 11:23) the same saying speaks of the power of faith being great enough to enable a man to tell a mountain to throw itself into the sea, while in Luke 17:5-6 a similar saying uses the illustration of a man with the merest grain of faith being able to tell a mulberry-tree to be uprooted and replant itself in the sea.

Moving mountains and planting trees on the bed of the ocean are things which are obviously absurd and impossible. But, says Jesus, men with faith can do things which look just as absurd and impossible. In the great eleventh chapter of the Letter to the Hebrews we find a recital of what men of Israel were able to accomplish by their faith. But what is faith? Someone complained once that the word 'faith' is a marvellous let-out for parsons. When there is something or other in Christian teaching which is difficult to understand – or perhaps when the parson does not understand it himself –

he tends to say: 'This is a matter of having faith', as if faith were a magic ingredient which we throw into a mixture of reason, experience, tradition and scripture in order to make sense out of life.

But this is not at all what the author of the Letter to the Hebrews says about faith. He says faith means trusting in God despite all opposition and discouragement, venturing forward into the unknown future believing that God has a purpose for us and for the world, which in the long run he will accomplish despite all that the power of evil can do to thwart it. Or as Kierkegaard puts it: 'Faith consists in a man's lying constantly out upon the deep and with 70,000 fathoms of water under him.' Life is full of uncertainties, perils and hazards, and in such a world the author of Hebrews says to us that the only certainty is Christ. Faith means believing that he was right, even if the devil and all his agents keep telling us that he was wrong. A German theologian has said this: 'Faith is the assertion of a possibility against all probabilities. Such a faith has nothing else than Jesus Christ in the middle of a world which scoffs at all our hopes and fears.' Like St Paul, we must be prepared to be 'fools for Christ's sake' (1 Cor. 4:10).

The author of Hebrews in his catalogue in chapter 11 of Old Testament heroes who had the kind of faith that can move mountains, after mentioning great names like Abraham, Moses and David, lists those nameless heroes who maintained their loyalty to God through hardship, persecution and torture. He pictures them as taking part with us in the great race of life and together with us looking to Jesus, who himself has run the same race and reached the goal towards which we all strive, eternal life in the presence of God. But the story by no means ends with the Bible. Christian history highlights names like those of Francis of Assisi, William Booth, Wilberforce, Shaftesbury, Martin Luther King, Mother Teresa – social reformers, campaigners for racial equality, protectors of the underprivileged – who by their faith have moved mountains of hostility, indifference, antagonism and hatred. It is surely an honour and a privilege to be enrolled in this great pageant of the Church on earth and the Church in heaven, even if the mountains *we* can remove are merely molehills.

MARRIAGE AND DIVORCE

What God has joined together, man must not separate . . . Whoever divorces his wife and marries another commits adultery against her: so too, if she divorces her husband and marries another, she commits adultery (Mark 10:9, 11-12, NEB).

It is said that every third marriage in the USA ends in the divorce courts, and in this country present trends seem to point in the same direction. Many would argue that this is a healthier situation than in the days when stricter divorce laws condemned couples to be legally bound to each other for years after the marriage had ceased to be anything more than a façade. On the other hand, even the most eager advocates of easier divorce cannot but view with misgivings the effect of broken homes on young children and adolescents, with their toll of insecurity and consequent juvenile delinquency. Of course, as everyone knows, a happy home and a respectable upbringing are no guarantee that a teenager will not go off the rails, get into bad company and end up as a hippie or a drug-addict. Yet the evidence of the juvenile courts, social workers and one's own experience seems to point to the fact that a broken home is more often than not at the root of the trouble when young people become dropouts, or at best aimless drifters.

But if there are no children of the marriage and it has been entered upon purely as a legal contract, embarked on in a registrar's office, it must be difficult for husband and wife not to feel that, provided the law of the land permits it, a divorce is a matter which concerns only the two people involved, and that, if they find that for one reason or another they no longer wish to live together, the best plan is to end the marriage and to try again with someone else. This was more or less the practice in Old Testament times, except that according to Jewish law the dice were loaded against the wife, and while she could not divorce her husband. her husband could divorce her on the flimsiest of pretexts, such as that her cooking was not to his liking or that some other woman he fancied had a prettier face.

Jesus would have none of this, and when he was asked if it was lawful for a man to divorce his wife – a trick question which was intended to involve him in the legal wrangles of his day – he at once lifted the whole concept of marriage out of the realm of lawyers' arguments and placed it firmly on the highest possible plane, as a contract undertaken by two people in the sight of God. He is saying that there are three parties to any real marriage, a man, a woman and God. He goes back beyond Old Testament law to God's creation of men and women, and his purpose that in a new relationship with one another they should leave behind them the family circles in which they had been brought up, and become one person, not two, in a physical and spiritual unity for the total enrichment of their lives.

This companionship which is part of the purpose of God for his children is obviously intended to be companionship for life. Divorce is thus out of the question. This is what is meant by the words of Jesus: 'What God has joined together, man must not separate.' He is not talking about whether the law has the power to terminate a marriage. He places the onus on the man who contracts the marriage. It is he who must not separate the partners in a God-given union. In Jewish law it was only the husband who could do this, but as the next words indicate, embracing the practice in the non-Jewish world, the wife who divorces her husband is equally guilty of sin in the sight of God. In the parallel passage in Matthew 19:8 there is the notorious proviso: 'for any cause other than unchastity'. Most scholars regard this as a piece of Jewish legal casuistry, out of keeping with the whole spirit of Jesus' teaching here, and not originating from Christ himself. It was probably inserted by some Jewish Christian who felt that Jesus' standard was too high.

Indeed, it is for most people. Jesus is setting out the ideal of Christian marriage, not drafting legislation for the world and his wife. We cannot expect those who do not acknowledge that marriage is a sacrament, or at least an institution ordained by God, contracted in his presence and blessed by the Church, to treat it with the seriousness with which Christians must regard it. In an imperfect world the law of the land must make allowances for human weakness. But Christian men and women, as we know only too well, are also human and fallible. The Church must therefore uphold the Christian ideal of marriage as a lifelong companionship, and condemn divorce as contrary to the will of God as revealed in Christ, but the Church must not be guilty of the same 'hardness of heart' of which Jesus accused his countrymen. Its business in the case of a marriage which is heading for the rocks is reconciliation, not condemnation or repudiation. Christians must act in the name of the Church to do what they can to hold a marriage together for the sake of the children of the marriage and of the couple themselves, by sympathy, advice and understanding, remembering that the highest law of Christ is the law of compassion.

It would therefore be wrong for the Church, or for individual Christians, to deny a couple whose marriage, despite all efforts, has irrevocably broken down the prospect of happiness with another partner. Christ held up the ideal of companionship for life. It is no longer companionship if there is constant wrangling and bitterness for one reason or another. Things do not always turn out as we hope and plan, and if a marriage has reached the point of no return, common humanity, let alone Christian compassion, would leave the door open for a second chance – which is what the Bible tells us is God's way with his children.

THE MONEY PROBLEM

One thing you lack: go, sell everything you have, and give to the poor, and you will have riches in heaven; and come, follow me (Mark 10:21, NEB).

St Anthony of Thebes, brought up in a well-to-do Christian home, but orphaned at the age of eighteen, heard these words one day as part of the gospel reading in Church. He took them as a direct command of the Lord to himself and forthwith abandoned his comfortable existence, gave all his possessions to the poor and spent most of his life thereafter as a hermit in the Egyptian desert, attracting many others to follow his example. This was in the third century. About a thousand years later, St Francis of Assisi was equally moved by the same words and made them one of the rules of his order of preaching friars.

It has always been felt by some within the Church that this is the proper life for all Christians and that if we take our faith seriously we ought to treat these words of Jesus as literally binding on all his followers. But is this what Jesus intended? Let us look at this saying in its gospel context (Mark 10:17–27). Jesus, in company with his disciples, was on his way to Jerusalem, his last journey, which was to end on a cross. He was accosted by a stranger, who is described by Matthew as a young man, and by Luke as a member of the ruling class. After running up to him, the man knelt respectfully and, calling Jesus 'good Master', asked the searching question, 'What must I do to win eternal life?' Brushing aside the title of 'good Master' as pointless flattery and with a sharp reminder that only God should be called good, Jesus went on to answer the man's question.

'You know the commandments', he said, implying that

the way to life in the presence of God, which was what the man was concerned about, lay in keeping the Ten Commandments. Jesus proceeded to quote several of them, but as he later emphasized, they could be summed up in the two great commandments, to love God and our fellow-men wholly and utterly (Mark 12:28–31). The man's answer was that he had kept the commandments since he was a boy. Jesus fully approved of this and was instinctively attracted to him. But the man obviously felt that keeping the commandments had not brought him the peace of mind and the right relationship with God for which he was searching. His money had obviously come between him and God. As Mark tells us, when Jesus told him that there was one more thing he must do, sell everything he possessed and give it to the poor, and join the band of Jesus' disciples, 'his face fell and he went away with a heavy heart; for he was a man of great wealth'.

Jesus had put his finger on the man's problem and on his particular need – as it was later to be in the lives of St Anthony and St Francis. But it is not a summons to ordinary Christians today to embrace a life of 'holy poverty'. Few of us have great wealth. Many of us feel that our problem is rather to make ends meet. It would seem therefore that this saying of Jesus has little to teach us. But this is not so. The man in the story was not condemned by Jesus because he was wealthy. He was self-condemned because his wealth was his chief concern. On another occasion Jesus said: 'You cannot serve God and Money' (Luke 16:13, NEB), and the New Testament writers frequently warn us to beware of avarice. 'Do not live for money', says the author of Hebrews (13:5, NEB) and the first letter to Timothy tells us that 'the love of money is the root of all evil things' (6:10, NEB).

In the sequel to the story we have been considering, Jesus exclaims, 'How hard it is for those who trust in riches to enter the kingdom of God!' and follows it up with the memorable saying that 'it is easier for a camel to pass through the eye of a needle than for a rich man to enter the kingdom of God'. Not surprisingly, the disciples were astounded. Had not Abraham been a wealthy man, and the pious Job, they must have wondered. But Jesus' last word on the subject makes his meaning plain. Wealth makes it difficult for a man to be in the right relationship to God, but not impossible. The grace of God can move a man to use his wealth for the good of others. History is full of examples of rich men who have treated their money as a servant and not made it into a god. Hospitals, schools, churches, medical research, libraries, art galleries and countless good causes testify everywhere to the generosity of those who have devoted their wealth to the glory of God.

But wealth is relative, and we cannot escape our obligations by claiming – as most of us could – that by no stretch of the imagination could we be described as wealthy. Yet, by the same token, the citizens of the Western world are rich beyond the dreams of avarice in the eyes of the other two-thirds of mankind who live on the border-line of starvation. Press reports of spending sprees on luxury goods, and the hectic pursuit of the pot of gold at the end of the rainbow via football pools or premium bonds are equally repulsive to the Christian conscience. Stewardship of such money as we have is part of our Christian service, neither to hoard it nor to throw it away.

In the welfare state much of our income goes through taxation to help the underprivileged, the old and the sick. The tax system is a fair and reasonable way of fulfilling much of our Christian obligation to the community of which we are members. But we have also, as members of the Church, an obligation to support its work as well, and to give generously, as far as our means allow us, to the variety of good causes outside the Church which invite our help.

Glory to God in the Highest.
And on Earth?

J. C. O'Neill

Decide the text and meaning of the angels' song in Luke 2:14 and you have decided the content of the worship of millions of ordinary Christians who say the *Gloria*. That has always been so. Formerly, the decisions divided Christians, so that Roman Catholics said, '*Gloria in excelsis Deo, et in terra pax hominibus bonae voluntatis*', and other English-speaking Christians, 'Glory be to God on high, and in earth peace, good will towards men.' Now, through the International Consultation on English Texts, there will almost certainly come into use a common agreed version. This bland, colourless version is meant to represent the view of Luke 2:14 which was first authoritatively proposed in the Revised Version, and which has recently received great support from both Protestant and Roman Catholic New Testament scholars:

Glory to God in the highest,
And on earth peace among men in whom he is well
 pleased.

I very much fear that this is the wrong decision, and I give the following arguments in honour of Professor William Barclay, who has done more than most New Testament scholars to keep open the traffic between scholars who argue – who must argue – about words, and ordinary Christians who simply want help to pray and to live. My particular solution could hardly be adopted in worship, but I hope that my

arguments will strengthen the hands of those who are loath
to lose the good sense and good theology of the old English
translation, 'Glory be to God on high, and in earth peace,
good will towards men.'

I wish to discuss five ways of taking the verse, four of which
have some support in the textual tradition.

First, there is the version which is found in the Syriac
manuscripts. They read καί for ἐν, and read εὐδοκία.
(Luther intuitively adopted this form, without knowing of
any direct manuscript support.) It has three distinct parts:

1st colon: Glory to God in the highest;
2nd colon: And peace on earth;
3rd colon: And favour to men.

Unfortunately there is no support in the Greek manuscripts for these readings, and we must conclude that it is a
paraphrase of the second version. This is found in the
correctors to ℵ and B, in Θ, in families 1 and 13, in the
Byzantine tradition as a whole, and in all the Greek fathers,
with the exception of Origen (and even he has it three times).
These witnesses follow our printed texts down to the last
word, where they read εὐδοκία.

Those who follow this version probably understood the
song as divided into three cola:

1st colon: δόξα ἐν ὑψίστοις θεῷ
2nd colon: καὶ ἐπὶ γῆς εἰρήνη
3rd colon: ἐν ἀνθρώποις εὐδοκία

There is one little-noticed fact which counts in favour of this
interpretation. When εἰρήνη is used in the phrase 'peace
upon so-and-so', it is usually followed by either the dative or
the preposition ἐπί. The phrase εἰρήνη ἐν occurs at Luke
12:51; 19:38; John 16:33, of which only Luke 19:38 is at all
parallel, but even here the meaning is not 'peace upon

so-and-so' but 'peace in a place, in heaven'. After the natural construction δόξα θεῷ, one might have expected the equally natural εἰρήνη ἀνθρώποις, if the word 'peace' did in fact go with 'men'. In other words, ἐν ἀνθρώποις in the Byzantine texts does relate more easily to εὐδοκία than to εἰρήνη, especially since we have ἐν σοὶ εὐδόκησα in Luke 3:22 (cf. Ps. 147(146):11).

However, there is one almost insuperable objection to accepting this reading. We could have translated the Byzantine text satisfactorily in three parts if there were either no καί at the beginning of the second colon, or a καί at the beginning of the second and third cola.[1] As it stands, this interpretation in three cola is forced. Ropes's suggested full stop after εἰρήνη is of little help, since the 'peace on earth' and the 'good will to men' are closely related.

The third reading is supported by the first hands of ℵ and B, and by A, D and W. These manuscripts have taken the song as a couplet in parallelism, which is what the psalm-like language would make us expect. The first colon,

δόξα ἐν ὑψίστοις θεῷ,

has three parts, referring to the gift, the place where it is received, and the recipient. The second colon is:

καὶ ἐπὶ γῆς εἰρήνη ἐν ἀνθρώποις εὐδοκίας,

referring to the place of reception (on earth), the gift (peace) and the recipients (ἄνθρωποι εὐδοκίας).[2]

There are three initial objections to the reading of ℵ*, B*, A, D and W, all based on the fact that ἐν ἀνθρώποις εὐδοκίας is a very awkward phrase.

First, the angels, I take it, are not announcing a fact but rather offering praise and peace. Even if we should understand an indicative of the verb 'to be' (as in 1 Pet. 4:11), the situation is not materially changed. What is, in the language of liturgy, is what should be, or what is offered. The angels are not stating a fact in the first part; they are offering God the glory due to his name. The same must be true in the second part. If the angels are praying for peace on earth, or proclaiming peace on earth, it seems awkward to begin to limit the men to whom it is available. The tone of the song suggests that peace is offered to all.

Second, Harnack has shown that there exists no real parallel in the Septuagint, Jewish literature, and early Christian literature to the expression ἄνθρωποι εὐδοκίας. He himself wishes to follow a hint of Hort's (and of Origen's), and to understand εὐδοκίας with εἰρήνη as εἰρήνη εὐδοκίας, supposing this to be a case of trajection or 'hyperbaton'. (He explains εὐδοκία as a variant introduced in recognition of the difficulty of ἄνθρωποι εὐδοκίας.) But clearly εὐδοκίας must be taken with its nearest noun, ἀνθρώποις, and that conjunction of words is every bit as difficult as Harnack makes out.

The difficulty is no longer in finding possible Hebrew or Aramaic phrases that could supply an original of which ἄνθρωποι εὐδοκίας was the translation: we now have from Qumran the Hebrew phrase 'all the sons of his favour' and the like (1QH IV. 32f.; XI.9; 1QS VIII.6), and the phrase in Aramaic, 'the man [=men] of [his] good will'.[3] The difficulty is in explaining how the supposed Semitic phrase could have been rendered into this Greek. Problems abound. As Frederick Field pointed out, the word for 'men' would naturally be ἄνδρες and not ἄνθρωποι.[4] If ἄνθρωπος were to be used, we should expect an article at least with the noun in the genitive, if not with both, as in ὁ ἄνθρωπος τῆς ἀνομίας (2 Thess. 2:3). In short, no one has yet produced an example of the Greek phrase ἄνθρωποι εὐδοκίας, nor an analogous example, and until one is produced, we must question whether Luke, or a translator from a Hebrew or Aramaic original, or a Greek speaker who was familiar with the Old Testament scriptures could possibly have written such a strange phrase as ἐν ἀνθρώποις εὐδοκίας.

Thirdly, the ἐν is awkward after εἰρήνη, as I argued earlier. This awkwardness is recognized by the Old Latin and part of the Vulgate tradition, with the support of a solitary minuscule, 372, and they omit ἐν. That is my fourth reading. This reading makes better Greek than the reading of our best uncials, but it is obviously a smoothing down of one difficulty.

But the same explanation – smoothing down of difficulties – clearly covers the third reading (of ℵ*, B*, D and W) and the first reading (of the Syriac). The reading which best explains the rest of the variants is the Byzantine:

δόξα ἐν ὑψίστοις θεῷ
καὶ ἐπὶ γῆς εἰρήνη ἐν ἀνθρώποις
εὐδοκία.

We have already seen that this can hardly be taken as three cola; we must take it as a couplet in parallel. The parallelism is perfect down to ἐν ἀνθρώποις, and the word left over is εὐδοκία. Εὐδοκία, however, cannot possibly be excluded from the original text, because it is intrinsically a stubborn word. It occurs very rarely in Greek outside Jewish writings, so we could hardly imagine a scribe's adding it to a sentence containing the common word εἰρήνη. Its position is also a little awkward, and likely to be original.

The best solution seems to be to take εἰρήνη as a gloss. Not only is it the more usual word, but it occurs in the very similar context at Luke 19:38:

ἐν οὐρανῷ εἰρήνη
καὶ δόξα ἐν ὑψίστοις.

I suggest that Luke originally reproduced a song which read:

δόξα ἐν ὑψίστοις θεῷ
καὶ ἐπὶ γῆς ἐν ἀνθρώποις εὐδοκία.

A glossator put εἰρήνη in the margin against εὐδοκία, from where it was later copied into the text, in what seemed its only possible position; there the word 'peace' has been causing trouble ever since. It has driven a wedge between ἐπὶ γῆς and ἐν ἀνθρώποις and raised the question of whether καὶ ἐπὶ γῆς should not be read with the first line. It has pushed εὐδοκία out on a limb, and suggested the superficially attractive but disastrous emendation εὐδοκίας.

When the Reformation era went back behind the Latin to the Greek, they found a text which in fact was closer to the original than the Latin, and they divided the song into three to get tolerable sense. The older manuscripts we now employ have raised the possibility that the Latin tradition was right after all, but this, I submit, is a mistake. The text that explains all the others is the Byzantine reading, yet all the others provide evidence that the Byzantine reading could not have been what Luke wrote. The word εἰρήνη is a gloss.

The song was originally the offer of God's good will and favour to all men, the peace for which all men long. We should do nothing in our worship to suggest otherwise.

New Testament Christology in a Pluralistic Age

George Johnston

I

As I have reflected on the subject of this essay I have found myself thinking of the great oil rigs now to be found in the North Sea off the coasts of Scotland and Norway, in the Gulf of Texas, offshore from Nova Scotia, and in many other maritime areas. Previous surveys have indicated the likelihood that there may be some of the rich rare stuff down at the bottom of the sea, so the rigs are in place to exploit the potential and bring in the benefits and the fat profits.

When one wants to consider the Christian faith in the context of the present world, a world which is ever more pluralistic in religion, to compare it with competing faiths and with the concepts obtaining in philosophy or the sciences, one knows in advance from many surveys that the canon of the scriptures is bound to be happy hunting-ground. For it has unrivalled authority as the source for truth as understood by Christian believers. Despite the way in which literary and historical critics have messed it up with their probing, analytical investigations, it remains the canon, the standard. Scholars like Professor Northrop Frye of Toronto, perhaps the most distinguished literary critic in Canada and an ordained minister to boot, can demonstrate how marvellously the whole Bible, and not simply the New Testament, is governed by a common symbolism: how the powerful images of the garden, the city, the temple, the tree and the river (to name a few) continue to recur and so give this incomparable literature a very impressive unity. Those who can go beyond the literary and imaginative beauty to accept the fundamental religious message contained in the scriptures find themselves being constantly fed and refreshed as they let themselves fall under the spell of the myths, the legends, the histories, and the letters, to say nothing of the apocalypses, that make up the Bible.

It is, of course, in the four Gospels that one finds the true biblical centre, because for Christians the Hebrew writings they call the Old Testament are held to find their fulfilment in the story of Jesus, the mediator of a new and better covenant (cf. Heb. 8:6f.). 'You search the scriptures', says the Johannine Jesus to the Jews, 'because you think that in them you have eternal life; and it is they that bear witness to me' (John 5:39). 'Your father Abraham rejoiced that he was to see my day; he saw it and was glad . . . Truly, truly, I say to you, before Abraham was, I am' (John 8:56, 58).

Indeed, one might well plunge into the question whether an exclusive-truth claim for the Christian message is still possible in a pluralistic age by seeing how the Fourth Evangelist dealt with such an issue in his own time. It is he who seeks to promote faith in Jesus as 'the Christ, the Son of God', so that as believers men and women may enjoy 'life in his name' (John 20:31). His Jesus says bluntly, 'I am the light of the world' (9:5) and 'I am the way, and the truth, and the life' (14:6).

But I have chosen rather to sink two shafts into other New Testament material in order to see what comes up, and to reflect upon it.

2

The first consists of the speeches found in the first fourteen chapters of the Acts of the Apostles, centring on the text at 2:36: 'God has made him both *Lord* (*Kyrios*) and *Christ* (*Messiah*).'

Without entering into the critical problems about the date and authorship of Acts (*c.* AD 90, by someone not of St Paul's immediate circle, will do for our purpose), or the extent to which the reputed author Luke is to be regarded as a sophisticated theologian (he is in fact not at all systematic in his beliefs and he is pretty naïve), let me assume that the speeches are essentially 'Lucan' compositions but they are not simply to be dismissed as completely unfaithful to the ideas of the primitive Church.

The information that we pick up includes the following: There was a man, Jesus of Nazareth (or the Nasorean), to whom were ascribed 'mighty works and wonders and signs', i.e. amazing miracles. He had been crucified by lawless men at the instigation of the Jewish people and their leaders. He had, however, escaped death through the great miracle of resurrection and he had been exalted to 'the right hand of God'. Those who came to believe in him and in his future role as judge and ruler of men were washed in the water of baptism, experienced the divine pardon of their sins, and themselves became subjects of astonishing spiritual phenomena like 'speaking in other tongues', i.e. glossolalia, probably (this is the gist of Acts 2:22–38; cf. 3:20 and 10:42).

About half a dozen descriptions are found that bear on the assertion that this Jesus is *Christ*, i.e. *Messiah*, that strange figure of Jewish hope in the two centuries before the emergence of John the Baptist: for example, he is God's 'servant', 'the Holy One, the Just One', 'the Prince of life' (the meaning of *archēgos* in my view), and apparently the prophet who is predicted in Deuteronomy 18:15f., a second Moses to whom all Israel ought to listen (see 3:6, 13–15, 22; 4:26, 'the Lord's Anointed'; 5:42; 7:52; 9:22, Paul's message to Damascus after his conversion; 13:33–5, the fulfilment of promises made to the fabulous King David).

Right in the midst of the messianic material we come across a statement by the Apostle Peter which has been echoed and re-echoed as if it were the final, absolute truth about Jesus: 'This is the stone which was rejected by you builders, but which has become the head of the corner. And there is salvation in no one else, for there is no other name under heaven given among men by which we must be saved' (4:11f.).

When we seek to define more exactly this word 'salvation', we note the citation of Joel 2:32 at Acts 2:21: 'Whoever calls on the name of the Lord shall be saved.' In Joel the reference is to a dreadful day of divine judgement when some in Israel will be allowed to survive the chastening of the land and of the nations. In spite of the peculiar furniture of this apocalyptic proclamation, 'salvation' probably means liberation with a view to national peace and prosperity; and then the Lord God, Israel's God, will dwell in Zion (that is Jerusalem) and so Judah will be vindicated on earth.

Peter's tremendous claim is addressed by the author of Acts to the Jerusalem leadership and the Jewish nation as a whole. If only they will return to God and believe that Jesus of Nazareth is God's representative, they will find that in truth their messianic hope has come true and that the ultimate deliverance of their people is assured through the future part to be played by this same Jesus (cf. 1:11).

Now let me turn to the second title found in Acts 2:36: *Lord*, i.e. *Kyrios*.

It is common throughout the New Testament to find this word *Kyrios* employed both of Jesus and of Israel's God: see, for example, Acts 1:6, 21; 7:59f.; the words of the dying Stephen; 8:16, Samaritans baptized in the name of the Lord Jesus; and 9:5; 13:12; 14:22f.; 1 Corinthians 12:3; and Philippians 2:6-11.

Modern scholars usually hold that the *Kyrios* title was ascribed to Jesus as the One raised miraculously from the dead, so that it emphasizes his glory and exaltation in the divine realm. In Aramaic the same idea may appear in *Maran atha*. Older theologians like H. A. A. Kennedy were impressed that *Kyrios* is the LXX equivalent for the divine unspeakable name, the tetragrammaton, and suggested that this meant that Jesus was given divine honours almost from the very beginning of the Church's life. We need not discuss in detail the problems attaching to this matter.

3

What I find significant in this first probe is that we see early witnesses led by the Apostles Peter and John, later by Barnabas and Paul, who use various formulae in an effort to explain and commend Jesus. It is perhaps surprising how in the speeches of Acts the emphasis is on crucifixion and resurrection, while little evidence is provided to underwrite the claim that Jesus is the second Moses of Deuteronomy 18:15f. The explanation may well be that the teaching preserved in what we call the Gospel of Luke was intended to complement the post-resurrection gospel of the Jerusalem Church. It is also noteworthy that the Christians identified as the Lord-Messiah who will come one day to reign Jesus of Nazareth, a man consecrated by God, who had gone about in Galilee and Judea doing good and healing people who were oppressed by the devil (10:38; cf. 2:22).

The allusions to the second Moses, the Davidic Prince, and the gospel of 'God's Kingdom', all put the Nazarene movement in the context of Jewish Messianism. From the earliest Maccabean period (c. 165 BC) the messianic hope had been embedded in such concepts as the Covenant with Abraham, the Promise of Canaan, the Throne of David, the Agony and Vindication of the Servant of the Lord, the Day of Future Judgement, and finally the Emancipation of Israel to become the centre of a universal empire.

We should analyse that hope more precisely. It involved:

(a) *National purification*
This was a truly religious, and not merely a political and

economic, expectation. Hence the picture of a just ruler in Psalms of Solomon 17, the strict Essene discipline at Qumran, the eschatological baptismal rite of John the Baptist, and similar pietist movements within Judaism. The Jesus movement shared in the demand for repentance as a return to God, the Holy Lord, and for a life in obedience to him as Father rather than as Judge and Lawgiver (Matt. 5:1ff.).

(b) *National liberation*
Israel expected to be set free from Syrian or Roman bondage, and various groups were prepared to use whatever means were necessary to accomplish this. Jesus, however, was not willing (as I understand him) to employ violence in order to win Jewish freedom.

(c) *Holy war against spiritual powers*
It is in this light that I want to interpret Jesus' exorcisms (Mark 3:20–30). The sons of the Father are to overcome the forces of Satan and those who embody his wicked designs on men. There are parallels to such ideas in the Qumran doctrine of the Sons of Light led by their prince, the angel Michael, who must fight against the Sons of Darkness under the wicked angel Belial. The effects of victory are to be seen in restoration to health and sanity.

(d) *Establishment of a theocracy or a restored Davidic monarchy*
Jesus seems to have disclaimed the crudity of Davidic dreams (Mark 10:35–45; 12:35–7), but his followers did not always do so.

One must therefore be cautious about ascriptions of messianic language to the person and mission of Jesus; it could well be that we distort his message altogether if we associate it with even the moderate hopes for an Israelite kingdom. Contemporary criticism of the Gospels should make us careful to avoid dogmatic statements, since the original teaching comes to us wrapped in the theological constructs of the Evangelists.

There is another significant result of our first probe into

the speeches in Acts. It is that *the interpreters of the Gospel were responding to exciting phenomena within their own communities.*

With his penchant for repetition, the author of Acts compels us to note pentecostal experiences at Jerusalem, at Samaria, at Caesarea, at Ephesus, and at many other centres of the Christian movement. These include speaking in tongues, healings, and other gifts of the Spirit, like inspired prophecy and courageous preaching. Jews exchanged a legalist religion for the freedom and grace of Jesus; Gentiles left the cults of polytheism and the mystery religions to accept Jewish monotheism and a faith that extraordinary events had taken place in Palestine. Luke himself may not have shared the expectation that the return of Jesus was imminent, but he does not leave out such an idea in his picture of the primitive churches. Life became different for those who confessed that God had sent Jesus and had raised him from the dead. In the Graeco-Roman and Persian worlds the Jesus movement had to define its gospel in the idioms of the Gentile culture. 'For although there may be so-called gods in heaven or on earth – as indeed there are many "gods" and many "lords" – yet for us there is one God, the Father, from whom are all things and for whom we exist, and one Lord, Jesus Christ, through whom are all things and through whom we exist' (1 Cor. 8:5f.).

The citation of Joel in the Pentecost speech put into the mouth of Peter (Acts 2) is typical of the way in which Christians made the Old Testament scriptures the substructure of their theology. They had precedent for this in the commentaries used at Qumran. Monotheism was accepted as the basic teaching of that scripture: 'I, the Lord, am your God and there is none else' (Joel 2:27). Hence the Christological problem of the apostolic Church was how to safeguard monotheism and yet assert that God had acted in and through Jesus of Nazareth to inaugurate the day of liberation, that is, the day of 'God's Kingdom'. The effort

led them by way of the *Logos* doctrine to the credal formulae
of Nicaea (AD 325) and Chalcedon (AD 451).

4

My second probe for oil begins with the enigma of the phrase
'*Son of man*' in the teaching of Jesus.

Everyone knows that, aside from one use in the words of
the dying Stephen (Acts 7:56), this phrase is confined to the
lips of Jesus himself. It appears in the Gospel of John but not
elsewhere in the New Testament, perhaps because in Greek
it is almost beyond comprehension. It has been suspected by
some scholars, with reason, that substitutes for 'Son of man'
may be found in later material like 1 Corinthians 15:45,
'the Last Adam', and Colossians 3:9f., 'the old *anthropos*' and
the new. It is well-known too that the Psalter contains 'Son
of man' references: for example, 'What is man that thou art
mindful of him, and the son of man that thou dost care for
him?' (Ps. 8:4), and, 'Let thy hand be upon the man of thy
right hand, the son of man whom thou hast made strong for
thyself' (Ps. 80:17); but are these examples to be taken as
use of a title? In Ezekiel the prophet is addressed as 'Son of
man' (2:1ff.), and in Daniel 7:13 there occurs the most
famous case, where 'one like a son of man' came with the
clouds of heaven before the Ancient of Days and received
'dominion and glory and kingdom', i.e. a universal empire.
At 7:27 this seems to be made less cryptic in the promise of
this empire to 'the people of the saints of the Most High',
which is clearly the people of Israel, the holy nation. Other
examples of 'Son of man' are found in the Similitudes of
Enoch, whose date is uncertain and disputed.

Some of the examples show that 'Son of man' is merely a
synonym for 'man'; but the problem is why 'man' seems to
have a technical meaning and to be associated with the
apocalyptic dreams of the Book of Daniel.

Aramaic background has long been sought, and we now

have a very significant discussion by Geza Vermes in appendix E to the third edition of Matthew Black's magisterial *An Aramaic Approach to the Gospels and Acts*.[1]

The Hebrew for 'Son of man' is *ben adam*; in Aramaic it is *bar nash* or *bar nasha*. Jesus probably spoke Aramaic, and enough Galilean material from about his time is available now to assist us. Vermes proves that the phrase 'Son of man' can be a circumlocution for 'I'; although it seems to me that the evidence he cites allows also for the translation 'a man' in certain cases. At any rate, we must take some of the 'Son of man' sayings in the teaching of Jesus as referring to himself: for example, in Q, 'The Son of man has come eating and drinking . . .' (Luke 7:34; Matt. 11:19). They must not, however, be forced into a collective sense as in Daniel 7, referring to Israel or the community composed of Jesus and his disciples, unless such a meaning is imperatively demanded by the context. (Interpretations along this line are, of course, not original with Vermes.)

There is no good reason to doubt that Jesus may have spoken about himself and his mission in sayings like Mark 10:45, 'For the Son of man also came not to be served but to serve, and to give his life as a ransom for many' (the word 'many' here may be technical for 'the congregation', i.e. Israel as a corporate entity, as Joachim Jeremias has said, with support from Qumran usage). Or Luke 19:10, an L text, 'For the Son of man came to seek and to save the lost.' We should note here the verdict on Zacchaeus, 'Today salvation has come to this house, since he also is a son of Abraham.' Zacchaeus really becomes part of the family of Abraham, a son of the Covenant or a son of the 'Kingdom', when he opens his hands and his heart to his fellow-men through the encounter with Jesus. That is what happens when Jesus comes, according to the presentations of all the Evangelists. Ancient hopes came true; new prophecies commended themselves to those who were ready to hear his new word. Disciples then went out, 'sent' by Jesus even as he had been 'sent' by God his Father, to tell this good news to Israel (Mark 6:12f.; Matt. 10:5–15; with echoes of the Second Isaiah). The redemptive mission defined in such sayings had to end in passion and death, for Jesus had to share the fate of God's other prophets of a like salvation.

This conclusion comes from multiple Synoptic sources; it is not the exaggeration of any one of them; it is like and yet unlike contemporary Jewish discussions about divine acts of salvation and liberation, for Ezekiel and Daniel were certainly not ignored among the various sects and parties in the Judaism familiar to Jesus. It is, on the other hand, not required that we base Jesus' own convictions solely on Isaiah 53 or on 1 Enoch.

Besides 'Son of man' sayings referring to the present time or to suffering, there are others, also of multiple attestation, that refer to the future:

In Mark: 'And Jesus said, "I am [the Son of the Blessed]; and you will see the Son of man seated at the right hand of Power, and coming with the clouds of heaven" ' (14:62, words strongly reminiscent of Pss 80 and 110, and of Dan. 7).

In Q: 'For the Son of man is coming at an unexpected hour' (Luke 12:40; Matt. 24:44).

'For us the lightning flashes and lights up the sky from one side to the other, so will the Son of man be in his day' (Luke 17:24; Matt. 24:27).

As it was in the days of Noah,
so will it be in the days of the Son of man.
They ate, they drank, they married, they were
   given in marriage,
until the day when Noah entered the ark,
and the flood came and destroyed them all . . .
so will it be on the day when the Son of man is
   revealed (Luke 17:26–30; Matt. 24:37–9,
   though the latter omits the second stanza
   of this powerful poem).

In L: God will vindicate his elect. 'Nevertheless, when the Son of man comes, will he find faith on earth?' (Luke 18:8).

It is not easy to relate these sayings to the mission and ministry of Jesus.

To say that Jesus is speaking of another, an eschatological figure of the future time, is just too simple a way out of our dilemma. To throw up our hands and ascribe all this to the theology of the primitive Church, or else to find Jesus guilty of gross miscalculation, has never solved all the puzzles. My own conviction is that Jesus believed that he himself was to be involved when the End arrived. He will be God's representative then, even as he was during his lifetime. But he knows not the day nor the hour (Mark 13:32, one of the sayings described as a pillar passage by Schmiedel in a famous article in the *Encyclopedia Biblica*[2]). It is possible, but by no means provable, that the visions of the resurrected Jesus granted to the first disciples, to James, to five hundred at once, and last of all to Paul (1 Cor. 15:5–8), were the fulfilment of Mark 14:62. At any rate, Jesus' 'exaltation to the right hand of God' is an article of faith throughout the New Testament period. (In much later times it has been taught that Jesus the Son of man 'comes' and 'comes again' in the eucharistic presence, in moments of conversion or ecstasy, at decisive turning-points in the history of the Church, and for individuals with assured faith at decisive and transforming experiences, even at marriage, at the birth of a child.)

What we must reflect on, from the bedrock sayings in which Jesus speaks cryptically about his function as that of the Son of man who came, who suffers, and who will come, is the deep conviction within them that Jesus claimed for himself *a unique prophetic authority*.

Without going into detail, which for thirty years I have had to probe over and over again, I have to confess that in my judgement now Jesus was really not interested in Davidic Messianism, or in Priestly Messianism. I think he may have accepted a vocation as the prophet of the new age, of that 'Kingdom of God' which is to be understood in our idiom as 'divine action in the history of Israel and the nations, in the exercise of sovereign, redemptive "power", i.e. the power of an eternal Love'.

Jesus was above all a teacher and a preacher: he taught (*pace* Bultmann) a fresh theology of Holy God as loving Father (the *abba*) (Luke 11:1ff.). Nothing except his own charisma, his revolutionary theology, the consistency of his acts with his words, can begin to explain the impact and extension of the Jesus movement and its continued vitality.

Hence I want still to make room for the remarkable Q saying in which Jesus refers to himself as 'the Son', the Son *par excellence*: he has a unique prophetic duty to be the representative of God in his saving act, to be his Son (in the Semitic use of that word). 'All things have been delivered to me by my Father; and no one knows who the Son is except the Father, or who the Father is except the Son and any one to whom the Son chooses to reveal him' (Luke 10:22; Matt. 11:27; cf. Mark 12:6f.; and the many examples of the Son in Paul and the Fourth Gospel).

Such a claim is at least in part an exclusive one. But the context of Palestine under Roman occupation; the context of Judaism split among Essenes, Sadducees, Zealots and Pharisees on the exegesis of divine wisdom and divine plans for the inauguration of a new time of liberation for Israel among the nations; and the context of Jesus' personal communion with God, are all factors to be reckoned with: and we must not jump from his exclusive mission in the first century to an exclusive claim for him in the different age of our own pluralistic, twentieth-century world without quite careful thought. He may indeed continue to be somehow (through the one dynamic spirit that is divine?) the single mediator to us of Love in God as the clue to our destiny; but we should need far more evidence than the records of the New Testament alone to persuade us, in spite of the status of those records as part of a canon.

At the same time, it is astonishing to see from the examples in Vermes's appendix to Black's book how the 'Son of man' phrase in Aramaic usage often carried with it a *self-effacing modesty*. Thus it is employed once about Abraham when he is made to claim that he possesses the holy spirit (i.e. the spirit of God). The conviction grows on me as an exegete of the Gospels that a profound humility was characteristic of Jesus of Nazareth; he did not go around Galilee saying that he was divine, far less that he was God. But there is just enough evidence, as I tried to show almost twenty-five years ago in the article 'Spirit' in Alan Richardson's *A Theological Word Book of the Bible*,[3] to demonstrate that Jesus might well have said too that the Holy Spirit was in him (see Mark 3:29f.).

Afterwards the Church proceeded to think out what it meant to believe that in Jesus (not only as crucified, but as living Lord also) God had inaugurated the new age. It was natural for many to put this in futuristic messianic categories; sometimes to combine priestly, prophetic and royal terminology, as in the so-called Epistle to the Hebrews. On occasion St Paul describes the Lord Christ as the *ikon* or image of God; and Paul or a disciple called him the *Prototokos*, the first-born in whom the whole pleroma of divinity was pleased to dwell (2 Cor. 4:4; Col. 1:15–20). But in Pauline theology God is the Head of Christ (1 Cor. 11:3); hence, at the End the sovereign Christ will hand over his kingship to God (1 Cor. 15:24).

It is in John's Gospel that the Christology goes yet further, for there Jesus Christ is the only Son (*monogenes*) and the *Logos* incarnate who is also a 'god' (John 1:1–14).

5

We have to recognize, therefore, that tremendous claims are made in the New Testament about the significance of Jesus; and yet the New Testament does not permit us to say bluntly that Jesus was interpreted as being God. Despite what the leaders of the World Council of Churches asserted in 1961, we cannot unite Christians on the basis of a faith that Jesus is God 'according to the scriptures'.

I suggest, with some trepidation, that in our modern pluralistic world the Christian claim for Jesus should be presented in considerable freedom from the trappings of Jewish Messianism dating from 165 BC to AD 135. When that is attempted, the emphasis will be placed on those elements of human perfection that are to be found in Jesus. We cannot claim omniscience for him, nor omnipotence. We have to accept, and accept with prideful joy, the fact that he was Jewish, because that was the historic form of his humanity (but today it is still by no means accepted adequately that Jesus was a Jew). If we are his disciples, we shall think it providential that this young prophet emerged from a pious, humble Jewish home where God was worshipped as the God of Israel. Perhaps Christians and Jews could begin to agree more than they do, if they could in common grant Jesus the status of a unique, prophetic representative of the one God.

One cannot argue for Jesus as scientist, philosopher, or even as scholar in the technical sense. On the other hand, he is wise as well as simple. He was a poet of profound perception, a superb story-teller, a man of rare courage, faith, hope and love.

They are truly his disciples who have to confess that he is the person (attested in scriptures) in whom and through whom they have found *God* present to their hearts and minds, present to win them to loving as the way of life, present to drive them to abject penitence, present to inspire their entire loyalty; the person whose gospel story enables them over and over again to rediscover God and their duty to serve him alone.

Hence it has to be said, even in this pluralistic age, that men and women, Christians or not, must learn *to give Jesus his due*. But that has to be done in his own spirit, and therefore graciously, not dogmatically but reasonably. It need not involve us in casting aspersions on others who are offered to the world as prophets or gurus. Rather, we Christians have to be contrite if we or our predecessors have given offence, however unwittingly, by an imperialist evangelism or theology or ecclesiasticism. For judgement always begins at our own door, if we are part of the house of God.

Even a student of New Testament Christology is driven, in the end, to state his own religious position; and so I have to declare in fear and trembling that Jesus is and he remains the supreme Word of God who commands my head, my heart, my will. I have had to think out his meaning, and go on re-thinking it, for two and forty years; with whatever intellectual rigour I can employ. For this Son of man forces on me, and, I believe, on all my contemporaries, the necessity of making sense of a world and of a history that contains his life and his death, his teaching and his influence. In fact, to hold that God was operative lovingly in him at all times does help me to give coherence to the human adventure, to make sense of all the tenses of time, to work day after day, in spite of the news from Ulster or Vietnam or Israel or Latin America or Equatorial West Africa, with the hope that to human life and to this universe there is a *telos*, a worthwhile goal, and that the issues of destiny are all safely in the control of that intelligence and goodness we call God the Father.

What I must never dare to hold is that the propositions in which such conclusions may have been enunciated in AD 325 or in 1560 or in 1932 or in 1974 are final; or that the ultimate truth about God and his Spirit and his Jesus is encased in them alone. Even our knowledge of the historic person, Jesus, can be presented only with probability; for that is the nature of historical science. God alone is ultimate, not theology, not Christology. The love in Jesus and the sacrificial goodness he seeks from men and women are universal. That is not to be taken as a claim to truth which attempts to say the last word or to exhaust the entire mystery of faith.

Indeed, it would be presumptuous to offer any defence of the Jesus to whom New Testament Christology bears witness. For it is the Church that canonized the New Testament and the theologian who interprets that canon who are on trial before the world. Jesus is no longer on trial.

Cambridge Syriac Fragment XXVI

W. D. McHardy

This fragment is printed, without identification, as 'Fragment XXVI' in *Palestinian Syriac Texts*, edited by A. S. Lewis and M. D. Gibson.[1] It is a palimpsest, and, as Mrs Lewis explains in her introduction,[2] it 'formed part of the great collection of Hebrew parchments, so long stored in the Genizah of the synagogue in Old Cairo, which Dr Schechter received from the Grand Rabbi of Egypt in 1897. They were presented by him and by Dr Taylor, Master of St John's College, to the University of Cambridge in 1898.' The following is the description of the fragment given by the editors: 'A pair of conjugate leaves of fine vellum, a portion having been torn roughly away from the foot of both, much discoloured and wrinkled, with a few small holes. Maximum length $7\frac{1}{2}$ inches, breadth $5\frac{3}{4}$ inches . . . The under Syriac script is also in one column, and the re-agent has been used on it with advantage. A dirty water stain down the inner edges, where it is dangerous to use the re-agent, has prevented our reading the entire lines.'[3]

Although the name ܟܒ ܐܣܘܚܝܐ is clearly inscribed at the head of the Syriac on folio 1b, the Syriac underwriting of the palimpsest was first identified in a review of *Palestinian Syriac Texts* which appeared in *Deutsche Litteraturzeitung*,[4] where Professor V. Ryssel showed it to be the Peshitta text of 'Sirach, 13, 1–14, 1'.

Mrs Gibson, who deciphered the fragment for *Palestinian Syriac Texts*, misread this reference, for, in *Apocrypha Syriaca*,

Mrs Lewis records[5] that 'Mrs Gibson finds that Fragment XXVI is, as Professor Ryssel has pointed out, the Edessene Syriac text of Sirach xiii. 1–14'. She continues: 'It agrees closely with the text of Walton, so far as it is visible, and the script is very like that of Fragment XXX.' The Syriac script of Fragment XXX 'appears to belong to the fifth or sixth century'.[6]

The Syriac text of Fragment XXVI, as printed by Mrs Gibson, seems to consist of, at most, nineteen lines to the page. From an examination of the manuscript I have concluded that the number of lines to the page is twenty-one. Thus on folio 1a there are twenty lines which are more or less legible, and then one line with mere traces of writing. The twentieth line of folio 1b contains parts of the beginning of verse 13, and must have consisted of the first three words of that verse. But folio 2a begins thus: ܣ.ܠܝ, which is the ܣܟܠܘܬ of Lagarde's text. The three words ܕܚܠ ܢܩܘܦ ܐܢ which are thus unaccounted for would be the exact length of a line of the manuscript; they must have followed line 20 of folio 1b, but they are not now discernible owing to the disfigurement of the parchment. Thus folio 1b also had twenty-one lines of Syriac text. (This is apart from the heading ܟܬ ܐܣܡܚܐ, which appears to be a later addition; it is much clearer and darker, and it is separated from the Syriac text by a space the depth of two lines of the rest of the writing.) Similarly, it can be calculated that folio 2a also had twenty-one lines.

In order to illustrate those points and to provide a check on Mrs Gibson's decipherment, I append my transcription of folio 1a, b. Letters that are only partly legible I enclose in square brackets. At the foot of folio 1b I indicate by round brackets the line that, though no longer visible, must have stood there. I keep Mrs Gibson's half-brackets. From this transcription it will be seen that I have been able to add considerably to the amount that is decipherable.

The evidence for determining the textual affinities of

Fragment XXVI is very limited, but what there is indicates that the text is akin to that printed by Lagarde in *Libri Veteris Testamenti Apocryphi Syriace*. It may be set out in tabular form:

	Fragment XXVI	Walton
Sir. 13:2	‎ܐܘܡܠ]	‎ܠܡܪܐ
2	‎ܠܝ]	om.
4	‎ܠܗ]	om.

In all three instances the reading of Fragment XXVI has the support of Lagarde's text as well as that of the sixth/seventh-century Jacobite MS. B.M. 12142 and the sixth-century Jacobite Codex Ambrosianus. In the first and third entries Walton's text is supported by the Nestorian[7] and later Jacobite[8] MSS I have examined, while in the second, where the Nestorian MSS still agree with Walton, the later Jacobite MSS are now in agreement with Fragment XXVI and the earlier Jacobite witnesses, here supported by the ninth/tenth-century 'punctuation' MS. B.M. Add. 12178. Walton's readings have, of course, the support of the Paris Polyglot, for the Peshitta text in the London Polyglot is, with trifling changes, a reprint of the text given in the earlier edition.

CAMBRIDGE FRAGMENT XXVI

Sir. 13

	.	v. 2
	,].	
	.؟	
	.	
(5)		
		v. 3
	.؟	
(10)		v. 4
	؛	v. 5
(15)	..	v. 6
	.	
	..	
	..2.2.. ؛	v. 7
(20)	[	
	. . . . . .	

(Heading)	ܡܠܝ ܐܣܝܐ	
	ܘܗܢ ܡܕܟܣ . ܕܣܒܝ	v. 7 (cont.)
	ܘ.ܠܠ	
	. . . ܐ ܡܕܟܣ.	v. 8
	. .ܘܡܗܡܨ . ܠܠ	
(5)	.ܡܗܠܘ.ܐ. ܘܠܠ.	
	ܐ.ܠܚ ܟܘ ܚ. ܨܡܗܨ	v. 9
	ܨ ܠܠܨܡ .2 ܗܘ . .	
	ܨܒܨܨ. ܗ .ܠܚܘ.ܗ	
	ܕ. .ܐ.ܢܕܟ ܠܠ . ܕ	v. 10
(10)	. . . ܟܘܢ ܠܠ ܘܡ	
	ܠܚ ܠܠ ܐ.ܐ ܠܠ ܠܠ ܘܡܙ	v. 11
	ܠ . . ܠܠܟܡܗ] .	
	. . . ܠ.ܡ 2.	
	. . . ܗܡ .ܠܠܟܡܗ	
(15)	ܘܟ. .ܠܐ . .	
	.ܘܒܨܝ . . . ܐܟܘܨ	
	ܘ.ܗ2. . . ܠܠܘ.	v. 12
	.ܣܕ . . . ܗ	
	. . . .ܐܕܣ)	
(20)	. .ܘܗ ܙ . . .	v. 13
	(. . . . . .)	

Notes

THE BIBLE – WORD OF GOD?

1. Title of a volume by the Netherlands Reformed Church (English ed., SCM Press, London, 1969, with a warmly appreciative foreword by Professor Barclay).
2. Title of another lively volume in the recent debate about the Bible, by James D. Smart (Westminster Press, Philadelphia, 1970, and SCM Press, London, 1971).
3. J. I. Packer, *God has spoken* (Hodder & Stoughton, London, 1965), p. 13.
4. ibid.
5. See K. Barth, *Church Dogmatics*, esp. vols. I.i and I.ii (T. & T. Clark, Edinburgh, 1936 and 1956); and J. K. S. Reid, *The Authority of Scripture* (Methuen, London, 1957).
6. For a sympathetic statement, see J. Peter, 'Salvation-history as a Model for Theological Thought', in *Scottish Journal of Theology*, 1 (February 1970), pp. 1–12.
7. There is a powerful and moving exposition of Jesus' words as 'Word of God' in G. Bornkamm, *Early Christian Experience* (SCM Press, London, and Harper & Row, New York, 1969), pp. 4–6.
8. This type of position is well characterized, and some effective criticisms of it are made, in James Barr, *The Bible in the Modern World* (SCM Press, London, 1973), ch. III.
9. Barr, op. cit., p. 48.
10. ibid.
11. ibid.
12. C. F. Evans, *Is 'Holy Scripture' Christian?* (SCM Press, London, 1971), p. 16.
13. op. cit., p. 85 (Barr's italics).
14. ibid., p. 115.
15. ibid., p. 119; cf. pp. 117f., 128, 131.

16. J. Burnaby, *Is the Bible Inspired?* (SPCK, London, 1960), p. 109. This of course is not to deny that other genuine or alleged characteristics like apostolic authorship influenced the Church's decisions at later stages in the formation of the canon.

17. O. Cullmann, *Salvation in History* (SCM Press, London, 1967), pp. 136ff.

18. See, e.g., the vigorous exposition of this in Paul Lehmann, *Ethics in a Christian Context* (SCM Press, London, 1963), pp. 90–5.

19. There is no space in this essay to consider recent trends in exegesis which pay less attention to strictly historical factors than has been the case in most biblical work for at least the last century and a half. Techniques of literary criticism practised outside the biblical field have influenced works like Dan O. Via, Jr, *The Parables* (Fortress Press, Philadelphia, 1967). It is too early to say whether French structuralism will provide much light for biblical exegesis; a reading of *Analyse Structurale et Exégèse Biblique*, by R. Barthes and others (Neuchâtel, 1971), leaves me with more questions than answers.

20. *Westminster Confession*, I.1. It is an interesting exercise for members of the Church of Scotland today to consider just how much of this vital first chapter of the *Westminster Confession* on the Holy Scripture they can fully accept, and whether what they cannot accept is 'of the substance of the faith'.

21. On the 'forward thrust' of tradition, see D. Ritschl, 'A Plea for the Maxim: Scripture *and* Tradition', in *Interpretation*, xxv (1971), pp. 113–28.

22. The question of inspiration is so closely connected, at any rate in English-speaking circles, with that of inerrancy that it is difficult to separate the two. J. Burnaby (op. cit.) seeks to define inspiration by means of analogy from other types of inspiration. Modern Roman Catholic theology, in moving away from the old 'two-source' view of revelation (one source in scripture, one in tradition), tends to connect inspiration very closely with the creation of the Church (see, e.g., the *Dogmatic Constitution on Divine Revelation* of Vatican II, esp. chs II and III; and Karl Rahner, *Inspiration in the Bible* (Burns & Oates, London, 1961), p. 50).

23. Darton, Longman & Todd, London, 1970, p. 137.

24. op. cit., pp. 1–13.

THE OLD TESTAMENT – A QUESTION OF THEOLOGICAL RELEVANCE

1. op. cit. (Hodder & Stoughton, London, 1901), p. 72.
2. op. cit. (A. & C. Black, Edinburgh, 1881), p. vii.
3. Of these prophets George Adam Smith was to be the interpreter *par excellence*, particularly in his contributions to the Expositor's Bible, *The Book of Isaiah*, vol. 1 (Hodder & Stoughton, London, 1887), vol. 2 (1890); *The Book of the Twelve Prophets*, vols. 1 and 2 (Hodder & Stoughton, London, 1899).
4. op. cit., p. 109.
5. See J. D. Smart, *The Strange Silence of the Bible in the Church* (Westminster Press, Philadelphia, 1970, and SCM Press, London, 1971).
6. op. cit., vol. III, p. 197.
7. J. Moltmann, *The Theology of Hope* (SCM Press, London, 1967). A good introduction to the Pannenberg circle is to be found in A. D. Galloway, *Wolfgang Pannenberg* (Allen & Unwin, London, 1973).
8. e.g. Harvey Cox, *The Secular City* (SCM Press, London, and Macmillan, New York, 1965).
9. Penguin, Harmondsworth, 1971.
10. op. cit., p. 203.
11. ibid., p. 204.
12. In *Expository Times*, LXXXIII, 1 (October 1971), pp. 4–9.
13. In *Bulletin of the John Rylands Library*, 55 (1972), pp. 9–32.
14. ibid., p. 10.
15. ibid., p. 11.
16. Lynn White, 'The Historical Roots of Our Ecological Crisis', in *Science*, 3767 (10 March 1967). The relation between science and religious belief, both philosophically and empirically, is more complex and ambiguous than is often acknowledged. See, e.g., the very different approaches represented in *Science and Religious Belief*, ed. C. A. Russell (University of London Press, London, 1973).
17. op. cit., p. 5.
18. op. cit., p. 20.
19. ibid., p. 30.

20. ibid., p. 31.
21. ibid.
22. ibid.
23. ibid., p. 26.
24. W. C. Smith, *Questions of Religious Truth* (Gollancz, London, 1967), p. 119.
25. J. A. T. Robinson, in *Honest to God* (SCM Press, London, 1963), tilts at not a few windmills in this respect.
26. The monarchical model is criticized by Macquarrie, op. cit.
27. op. cit., p. 204.
28. ibid., p. 19.
29. ibid., p. 234.

A FUTURE FOR APOCALYPTIC?

1. Secker & Warburg, London, 1957.
2. See 1 Thess. 4:14–18.
3. Lutterworth Press, London, 1963.
4. See, e.g., the visions of the new Jerusalem in Revelation; cf. Dan. 7:14.
5. 3rd ed., A. & C. Black, London, 1963.
6. See J. Munck, *Paul and the Salvation of Mankind* (SCM Press, London, 1959).
7. See W. G. Rollins, 'The New Testament and Apocalyptic', in *New Testament Studies*, 17 (1971), pp. 454ff.
8. See, e.g., H. H. Rowley, op. cit.
9. Feine-Behm-Kümmel, *Introduction to the New Testament* (SCM Press, London, 1966), p. 333.
10. See the works of Hans Jonas.
11. Heinemann, London, 1973.
12. *Religion, Revolution and the Future* (New York, 1969), p. 218; see also *Theology of Hope* (SCM Press, London, 1967), pp. 37ff.

ESCHATOLOGY AND POLITICS: SOME MISCONCEPTIONS

1. *The Quest of the Historical Jesus*, 3rd ed. (A. & C. Black, London, 1963), p. 401.
2. *The Mission and Achievement of Jesus* (SCM Press, London, 1954), pp. 27–8.
3. *Promise and Fulfilment* (SCM Press, London, 1957), pp. 43–4.

4. *On Englishing the Bible* (Burns & Oates, London, 1949), p. 11.
5. Lutterworth Press, London, 1964.
6. Cambridge University Press, London, 1973.

NORTH AND SOUTH: TENSION AND RECONCILIATION IN
BIBLICAL HISTORY

1. 1 Kgs 12:1–24.
2. 'Kuthim' from one of the places of origin of the settlers in 2 Kgs 17:24, 30; 'lion-converts' from the story of 2 Kgs 17:25–8.
3. For a recent survey, see J. Macdonald, B. Tsedaka, A. Loewenstamm, article 'Samaritans', in *Encyclopaedia Judaica* (Jerusalem, 1972). The most important recent studies are J. Macdonald, *The Theology of the Samaritans* (SCM Press, London, 1964); J. Bowman, *Samaritanische Probleme: Studien zum Verhältnis von Samaritanertum, Judentum und Urchristentum* (Stuttgart, 1967); J. D. Purvis, *The Samaritan Pentateuch and the Origin of the Samaritan Sect*, Harvard Semitic Monographs, 2 (Harvard University Press, Cambridge, Mass., 1968); H. G. Kippenberg, *Garizim und Synagoge: Traditionsgeschichtliche Untersuchungen zur samaritanischen Religion der aramäischen Periode*, Religionsgeschichtliche Versuche und Vorarbeiten, XXX (Berlin, 1971).
4. See G. Fohrer, *History of Israelite Religion* (Abingdon Press, Nashville, 1972), pp. 60–2; J. Bright, *A History of Israel*, 2nd ed. (SCM Press, London, and Westminster Press, Philadelphia, 1972), pp. 126–33.
5. G. Fohrer, op. cit., pp. 68–74; J. Bright, op. cit., p. 130.
6. The tracing of the descent of the twelve 'sons' of Jacob/Israel through two wives, Leah and Rachel, and two concubines, Bilhah and Zilpah, suggests differences in status among the tribes at the outset.
7. The thesis of M. Noth, first presented in his *Das System der zwölf Stämme Israels* (Stuttgart, 1930), has been influential, but has come under increasing criticism of late. See G. Fohrer, op. cit., pp. 89–94. Nevertheless, some form of religious confederation is required to make sense of the period of the Judges.
8. See M. Noth, *The History of Israel*, 2nd ed. (A. & C. Black, London, 1960), pp. 91–4. Cf. the account of the renewal of the covenant under Joshua at Shechem in Josh. 24:1–28.

9. 1 Kgs 12:16; cf. 2 Sam. 20:1.
10. See the discussion in E. W. Nicholson, *Deuteronomy and Tradition* (Blackwell, Oxford, 1967), ch. IV, 'Deuteronomy and Northern Israel', pp. 58–82.
11. R. J. Coggins, 'The Old Testament and Samaritan Origins', in *Annual of the Swedish Theological Institute*, 6 (1967–68), pp. 35–48; J. Macdonald, 'The Structure of II Kings XVII', in *Transactions of Glasgow University Oriental Society*, 23 (1969–70), pp. 29–41.
12. 'The Samaritan Schism in Legend and History', in B. W. Anderson, W. Harrelson, eds., *Israel's Prophetic Heritage: Essays in Honour of James Muilenburg* (SCM Press, London, 1962), pp. 212, 213. The reference is to Ezek. 16:3, 45.
13. Ezra 4:1–5; Neh. 4, 6.
14. Against those who wish to date this in the Persian period, the Wâdī Dâliyeh finds have tipped the balance in favour of the accuracy of Josephus' chronology. Cf. J. D. Purvis, op. cit., pp. 98–105.
15. J. D. Purvis (op. cit.), on the basis of an examination of the script, orthography and text of the Samaritan Pentateuch, has concluded that the Samaritan tradition only diverged from the Jewish in the late Hasmonaean period.
16. Pss 46, 48, etc.
17. See B. W. Anderson, 'The Place of Shechem in the Bible', in *The Biblical Archaeologist*, 20 (1957), pp. 10–19.
18. See J. Macdonald, *The Theology of the Samaritans*, pp. 327–33.
19. Ps. 89:3, 4; 2 Sam. 23:1–7.
20. cf. B. W. Anderson, *Understanding the Old Testament* (Prentice-Hall, Englewood Cliffs, N.J., 1957), published in Great Britain under the title *The Living World of the Old Testament* (Longmans, Green, London, 1958), pp. 289, 290.
21. cf. M. L. Newman's analysis of the J and E covenant traditions, *The People of the Covenant: A Study of Israel from Moses to the Monarchy* (Carey Kingsgate Press, London, 1965), esp. p. 51.
22. Isa. 2:3; 60:14, etc.
23. J. Macdonald, *The Theology of the Samaritans*, p. 365.
24. See R. J. McKelvey, *The New Temple: The Church in the New Testament* (Oxford University Press, London, 1969), pp. 9–24.
25. Josephus, *Antiquities*, XVIII, 4, 1, attests this belief in the New Testament period.

26. Problems of authorship and date cannot be discussed here; see, e.g., G. Fohrer, *Introduction to the Old Testament* (Abingdon Press, Nashville, 1968), pp. 388–402. Editorial activity is not to be denied, but it was probably directed to toning down passages sympathetic to the North. On the whole subject, see H. W. Hertzberg, 'Jeremia und das Nordreich Israel', in *Theologische Literaturzeitung*, 77 (1952), pp. 595–602. Hertzberg wishes to assign the Northern oracles to the early period of Jeremiah's ministry. Irrespective of the modern discussion of authorship, it is important to remember that it was the book in its final (edited) form which influenced subsequent generations.

27. By J. Smith, *The Book of the Prophet Ezekiel: A New Interpretation* (SPCK, London, 1931), esp. ch. VI, 'Was Ezekiel a Prophet of the North?' Smith's thesis cannot however be accepted.

28. The concluding verse of the oracle (37:23) introduces the theme of the covenant: 'They shall be my people, and I will be their God.'

29. This point is argued by M. Gaster, *The Samaritans: Their History, Doctrines and Literature* (Oxford University Press, London, 1925), pp. 15, 138, 139. It was also maintained by C. Mackay in a long series of articles beginning with 'The City and the Sanctuary: Ezekiel XLVIII', in *Princeton Theological Review*, 20 (1922), pp. 399–417. Though Mackay's theory has not been accepted, the significance of a sanctuary some distance north of Jerusalem is noted by, e.g., J. Smith, op. cit., p. 66; S. Spiegel, 'Ezekiel or Pseudo-Ezekiel?', in *Harvard Theological Review*, 24 (1931), p. 373.

30. See C. Mackay, op. cit., pp. 414, 415.

31. Their teaching is echoed in the brief, post-exilic oracle incorporated at Isa. 11:11–16, and in Zech. 9:9, 10, 11–17; 10:6–12.

32. See K. Elliger, *Das Buch der zwölf kleinen Propheten*, vol. II, *Das Alte Testament deutsch*, 6th ed. (Göttingen, 1967), pp. 160–4; cf. M. Delcor, 'Hinweise auf das samaritanische Schisma im Alten Testament', in *Zeitschrift für die alttestamentliche Wissenschaft*, 74 (1962), pp. 281–91.

33. cf. Tobit 1:1, 2; Josephus, *Antiquities*, XI, 5, 2. Later Jewish tradition placed the ten tribes beyond a mysterious river 'Sambation'; see Targum Pseudo-Jonathan on Exod. 34:10;

Genesis Rabba 73. For the further development of these legends, see article 'Sambation', in *Jewish Encyclopedia*, X, pp. 681–3; E. Robertson, 'Notes and Extracts from the Semitic MSS. in the John Rylands Library: II. The Samaritans and the Sabbatic River', in *Bulletin of the John Rylands Library*, 20 (1935–36), pp. 354–78.

34. Testament of Moses 3:4–13; 4:9; 10:8, 9 (cf. R. H. Charles, *The Apocrypha and Pseudepigrapha of the Old Testament*, vol II (Oxford University Press, Oxford, 1913), p. 412); 2 Esd. 13; Apocalypse of Baruch 1:2, 3; 77:1–6; 78f. On this whole subject, see G. H. Box, *The Ezra-Apocalypse* (London, 1912), 'An Additional Note on the Ten Tribes', pp. 300, 301.

35. Sanhedrin 10:3; H. Danby, *The Mishnah* (Oxford University Press, Oxford, 1933), p. 398.

36. The original tradition of a translation by 70 men (based on Exod. 24:1, 9?) appears to have been altered to accommodate the theory of 6 men from each of 12 tribes. See M. Hadas, *Aristeas to Philocrates (Letter of Aristeas)* (New York, 1951), p. 72. This view is also reflected in Acts 26:6–7.

37. Acts 8:1–24. Luke's information on the Samaritan mission appears to have been very scanty. There are further brief references in editorial verses at 8:25; 9:31 and 15:3.

38. See, e.g., M. Dibelius, *Studies in the Acts of the Apostles* (SCM Press, London, 1956), p. 168; H. Conzelmann, *Die Apostelgeschichte*, Handbuch zum neuen Testament (Tübingen, 1963), pp. 50, 51.

39. The contributions of Plumptre, Hammer, Kahle, Wilcox, Spiro, Bowman, Scroggs, Scharlemann and Gaston are summarized in my article, 'The Origins and Development of Samaritan Christianity', in *New Testament Studies*, 19 (1972–73), pp. 390–414. Subsequent to the writing of this article, W. H. Mare published a critique of Spiro's essay ('Acts 7: Jewish or Samaritan in Character?', in *Westminster Theological Journal*, 34 (1971–72), pp. 1–21). Mare deals only with Spiro (Scharlemann's book is mentioned in footnote 4, but not discussed). His approach is determined in part by his 'conservative view of the inspiration of scriptures' (p. 5). He is rightly critical of many arguments advanced by Spiro, but he fails to undermine the main points which show a Samaritan source behind the speech.

40. Acts 3:12–26, though ascribed to Peter, appears to be based

on the same source as 7:2–53; there are many similarities
and Samaritan characteristics appear here also. Indeed,
Acts 3:12–26 (with due allowance for Lucan editing) would
make a very appropriate ending for the speech broken off at
Acts 7:53. Acts 22:14 also seems to be connected in some way
with the same source.

41. For a few possible allusions, see J. Grassi, 'Ezekiel XXXVII:
1–14 and the New Testament', in *New Testament Studies*, 11
(1964–65), pp. 162–4.

42. In 1 Cor. 11:25 it forms part of the tradition 'received' by
Paul.

43. It will be noted that this virtually reverses the thesis of E.
Lohmeyer (*Galiläa und Jerusalem* (Göttingen, 1956)), who
sees James as the leader of Northern or Galilean Christianity.

44. According to Luke 24:53; Acts 2:46; 3:1f.; 5:12; 5:42;
21:20f. James' praying in the Temple is mentioned by
Hegesippus, who also locates his martyrdom there (in
Eusebius, *Ecclesiastical History*, II, 23).

45. Rom. 1:3 probably cites a pre-Pauline formula incorporating
reference to Jesus' Davidic descent (one of the essentials of the
faith on which Paul and the Jerusalem leaders were agreed?).
One or both of the genealogies, proving Jesus' Davidic descent,
probably originated in Jerusalem, where Jesus' brothers and
mother were located (Acts 1:14).

46. Acts 7:37 cites Deut. 18:15. On this, see M. Simon, *St
Stephen and the Hellenists in the Primitive Church* (Longmans,
Green, London, 1958), pp. 59–63.

47. C. H. H. Scobie, op. cit., p. 397, n. 6.

48. Eusebius, *Ecclesiastical History*, III, 19–21, 32.

49. John 1:11. See C. H. H. Scobie, op. cit., pp. 403, 404.

50. e.g. Peter is *brought* to Jesus by the Hellenist Andrew (1:40–2);
he does not sit next to Jesus at the Last Supper. The Appendix (ch. 21), of course, seeks to reinstate Peter. In 7:1–9
Jesus' brothers do not 'believe in him'.

51. Jer. 31:10; Ezek. 34:11–16, 31.

52. Jer. 23:5; Ezek. 34:23, 24; 37:24.

53. cf. Jer. 10:21; 23:1–4; Ezek. 34:5, 6, 11–16.

54. The Gospel says nothing about an ingathering of the Gentiles;
cf. J. A. T. Robinson, 'The Destination and Purpose of St
John's Gospel', in *New Testament Studies*, 6 (1960), pp. 117–31.

55. 'Samaritan Studies, I: The Fourth Gospel and the Samari-

tans', in *Bulletin of the John Rylands Library*, 40 (1958), p. 302; *Samaritanische Probleme*, p. 56.

56. A similar idea occurs in John 11:52, with which compare Ezek. 37:21–2.
57. Ezek. 47:1–12; Zech. 13:1; 14:8; Joel 3:18.
58. cf. John 4:20–6.
59. For a survey of the work done in this area, see C. H. H. Scobie, op. cit., pp. 409–14.
60. cf. Heb. 7:14!
61. Heb. 3:1–19.

THE EPISTLE FOR TODAY

1. William Barclay, *The New Testament*, vol. II, *The Letters and the Revelation* (Collins, London, 1969).
2. In *Expository Times* (January 1972), p. 111.
3. The subjectivity of the meaning and content given to 'most wanted' and 'most needed' and also to the so-called 'contra-indications' in this exercise is as apparent to the writer as to the reader. We claim to offer one man's considered assessment – no more: certainly no infallible (or even surely impartial) judgement.
4. A. M. Hunter, *Romans* (SCM Press, London, 1955), p. 11.
5. A. M. Hunter, *Introducing the New Testament*, rev. ed. (SCM Press, London, 1957), pp. 96, 120.
6. Quoted in Y. Congar, *Tradition and Traditions* (Burns & Oates, London, 1966), p. 346.
7. R. P. Martin, *Broadman Bible Commentary*, vol. II (Marshall, Morgan & Scott, London, 1972), p. 125.
8. We put the situation thus because Ephesians too has 'justification' terminology. More generally, in our choice between Ephesians and Romans 'for today' we should remember that Ephesians presupposes, and specifically affirms, 'justification by grace through faith', in, e.g., Eph. 2:5, 8–9. In a sense, then, we have 'Romans-*plus*' in Ephesians.
9. cf. E. K. Lee's rewarding essay in *Studies in Ephesians*, ed. F. L. Cross (Mowbray, London, 1956).
10. If this be desired, however, it can be found admirably done in C. H. Dodd's analysis of Romans in his Moffatt New Testament Commentary volume, *The Epistle of Paul to the Romans* (Hodder & Stoughton, London, 1932).

11. On the present-day meaning to be drawn from Paul's use of first-century astrology and mythology, F. F. Bruce, 'St Paul in Rome. 3: The Epistle to the Colossians', in *Bulletin of the John Rylands Library*, 48, 2 (1966), pp. 284f., is particularly helpful. See also J. Y. Lee, 'Interpreting the Demonic Powers in Pauline Thought', in *Novum Testamentum*, XII (January 1970), pp. 54–68.

MARK 10:13–16: THE CHILD AS MODEL RECIPIENT

1. H. W. Kuhn, *Ältere Sammlungen in Markusevangelium* (Göttingen, 1971), pp. 146–91.
2. There is a useful summary on p. 187.
3. On the concepts 'following after' and 'imitation of', see H. D. Betz, *Nachfolge und Nachahmung Jesu Christi im Neuen Testament* (Tübingen, 1967); A. Schulz, *Nachfolgen und Nachahmen* (Munich, 1962).
4. See Best, 'Uncomfortable Words: VII. The Camel and the Needle's Eye', in *Expository Times*, 82 (1970–71), pp. 83–9.
5. There are many Marcan characteristics in v. 10: εἰς τὴν οἰκίαν, the private instruction of the disciples, the simple union with what preceded through καί, the use of πάλιν (linking back to previous private instruction) and ἐπερωτᾶν, probably influenced on this occasion by its use in v. 2.
6. op. cit., pp. 188f.
7. See Best, 'Mark's Preservation of the Tradition', in *L'Evangile selon Marc*, ed. M. Sabbe (Gembloux, 1974), pp. 21–34.
8. op. cit., pp. 53–146.
9. Since Kuhn, op. cit., pp. 32–6, does not accept 9:35–50 as a pre-Marcan collection, it would have been easy for Mark to include 10:13–16 as he compiled it. If Mark received it and only modified it, then he could still have inserted 10:13–16 or placed it directly after 9:50.
10. cf. K. G. Reploh, *Markus – Lehrer der Gemeinde*, Stuttgarter Biblische Monographien, 9 (Stuttgart, 1969), pp. 163ff.; S. Légasse, 'Approche de l'Episode préévangélique des Fils de Zébédée (Marc x: 35–40 par.)', in *New Testament Studies*, 20 (1973–74), pp. 161–77.
11. M. Smith, *Clement of Alexandria and a Secret Gospel of Mark* (Harvard University Press, Cambridge, Mass., 1973).
12. For a thorough examination of Smith's views, see now H.

Merkel, 'Auf den Spuren des Urmarkus? Ein neuer Fund und seine Beurteilung', in *Zeitschri fürft Theologie und Kirche*, 71 (1974), pp. 123–45; W. Wink, 'Jesus as Magician', in *Union Seminary Quarterly Review*, 30(1974), pp. 3–14; R. E. Brown, 'The Relation of "The Secret Gospel of Mark" to the Fourth Gospel', in *Catholic Biblical Quarterly*, 36(1974), pp. 466–85.

13. For this summary, see Smith, op. cit., p. 187.
14. op. cit., pp. 186f.
15. Smith, op. cit., p. 170, denies the validity of the examples in Acts, alleging that the argument for the absence of pre-baptismal instruction in Acts is drawn from silence – but from where else could it be drawn? Clearly the author of Acts could not have been expected to insert a footnote: 'For the benefit of later generations it must be noted that there was no pre-baptismal instruction'!
16. op. cit., pp. 186f.
17. See n. 10.
18. A. Isaksson, *Marriage and Ministry in the New Temple* (Lund, 1965), pp. 119, 121.
19. Put more accurately, Isaksson argues that Matt. 19:1–15 forms the catechism; its existence would prove that Mark 10:1–16 was a pre-Marcan unit.
20. cf. H. Baltensweiler, *Die Ehe im Neuen Testament* (Zürich, 1967), p. 59; B. H. Streeter, *The Four Gospels* (Macmillan, London, 1936), pp. 259–61; B. K. Didericksen, *Den markianske skilsmisseperikope* (Gyldendal, 1962), pp. 116ff.; D. Daube, *The New Testament and Rabbinic Judaism* (Athlone Press, London, 1956), p. 71; J. Schmid, 'Markus und der aramäische Matthäus', in *Synoptische Studien*, Festschrift für A. Wikenhauser (Munich, 1953), pp. 148–83, esp. pp. 177ff.
21. J. Jeremias, *Infant Baptism in the First Four Centuries*, ET by D. Cairns (SCM Press, London, 1960), p. 50; cf. E. Schweizer, *The Good News according to Mark* (SPCK, London, 1971), pp. 201f.; S. Légasse, *Jésus et l'Enfant* (Paris, 1969), pp. 36f., 206–18; W. Grundmann, *Das Evangelium nach Markus*, 3rd ed. (Berlin, 1968), p. 201.
22. Baltensweiler, op. cit., p. 73, goes much further in regarding all that lies between the second and third passion predictions (9:33–10:31) as originally a pre-Marcan complex which

Mark has modified and added to. Mark 9:33-50 does not appear to have any real homogeneity with 10:1-31.

23. We shall see later that the addition of v. 15 has changed this pericope.

24. See below.

25. See Best, as in n. 4.

26. cf. C. H. Turner, 'Marcan Usage', in *Journal of Theological Studies*, 25 (1924), pp. 378ff.

27. e.g. Wohlenberg, *Das Evangelium des Markus* (Leipzig, 1910), p. 272.

28. The idea of movement is confirmed by the use of ὁδός throughout the discipleship section, 8:27-10:52.

29. cf. Reploh, op. cit., pp. 186ff.

30. 15 times in Matthew, 3 in Mark, 4 in Luke.

31. Mark did not create the theme (cf. 9:18f.; 10:35ff.) but developed it; cf. Kuhn, op. cit., p. 182.

32. cf. Bultmann, *The History of the Synoptic Tradition* (ET, Blackwell, Oxford, and Harper & Row, New York, 1963), p. 32; Légasse, *Jésus et l'Enfant*, p. 38, n. 20; J. Jeremias, 'Mc 10: 13-16 Parr. und die Übung der Kindertaufe in der Urkirche', in *Zeitschrift für die neutestamentliche Wissenschaft*, 40 (1941), pp. 243-4; J. I. H. McDonald, 'Receiving and Entering the Kingdom. A study in Mark 10:15', in *Studia Evangelica*, VI (=*TU* 112), pp. 328-32.

33. cf. the argument of Légasse, *Jésus et l'Enfant*, p. 43. Matthew certainly does not dislike doublets and would not necessarily omit v. 15. Possibly he knew the incident in his oral tradition as well as in its written form in Mark; because his oral form did not include v. 15, and because he had already used a close variant at 18:3, he dropped it in his parallel to Mark 10:13-16.

34. It is not original to the context of Matt. 18:1-5, as the change of number there shows; however, it is extremely unlikely that if Matthew found it in the singular in Mark 10:15, which is the number in 18:1, 2, 4, 5, he would then change it into the plural in order to transfer it; moreover, the other variations do not suggest changes on his part from the Marcan form; cf. Légasse, *Jésus et l'Enfant*, pp. 33-5; W. L. Knox, *The Sources of the Synoptic Gospels*, vol. II (Cambridge University Press, London, 1957), p. 16, n. 1; A. M. Ambrozic, *The Hidden Kingdom*, Catholic Biblical Quarterly Monograph, II (Catholic

Biblical Association of America, Washington, D.C., 1972), pp. 136–8. The contrary view is argued by W. G. Thompson, *Matthew's Advice to a Divided Community, Matt. 17:22–18:35,* Analecta Biblica, 44 (Rome, 1970), pp. 76–8, 136f.

35. cf. C. H. Dodd, *Historical Tradition in the Fourth Gospel* (Cambridge University Press, London, 1963), pp. 358f. We are not concerned to trace whether the saying goes back to the historical Jesus; cf. Légasse, *Jésus et l'Enfant,* pp. 187f.

36. The origin of vv. 13, 14ab, 16 need not detain us; they were certainly not composed as a setting for v. 15 (cf. Bultmann, op. cit., p. 32).

37. The reception and blessing would not be exceptional in a Jewish context; cf. J. Jeremias, op. cit. (see n. 21), p. 49; H. L. Strack and P. Billerbeck, *Kommentar zum Neuen Testament aus Talmud und Midrasch* (Munich, 1922–28), vol. I, pp. 807f.

38. cf. Moulton-Turner, *Grammar of New Testament Greek,* vol. III (T. & T. Clark, Edinburgh, 1963), pp. 46f.; Légasse, *Jésus et l'Enfant,* p. 39; F. W. Blass and H. Debrunner, *Greek Grammar of the New Testament,* trans. R. W. Funk (Cambridge University Press, London, 1961), § 304.

39. Jeremias, op. cit. (see n. 21), p. 49, takes it in the sense, the 'Kingdom belongs *also* [our italics] to children'; but *also* is neither present in the text nor clearly implied by the context.

40. cf. C. H. Turner, 'Marcan Usage', in *Journal of Theological Studies,* 26 (1925), pp. 145–56; M. Thrall, *Greek Particles in the New Testament* (Leiden, 1962), pp. 41ff.; C. H. Bird, 'Some γάρ Clauses in St Mark's Gospel', in *Journal of Theological Studies,* 4 (1953), pp. 171–87.

41. On Matthew's treatment of v. 15, see n. 33. Even if v. 14c was not in his oral form, he would have retained it here because it still makes the point without v. 15 and because, unlike v. 15, he did not have a parallel to it elsewhere.

42. The Greco-Roman world idealized the mature adult; in Judaism the child was 'weak' and not expected to keep the law until he became bar-mitzvah; cf. A. Oepke, in *Theological Dictionary of the New Testament,* ed. G. Kittel and G. Friedrich, trans. G. W. Bromiley, IV, p. 916; V, pp. 639–48; Billerbeck, vol. I, pp. 569f., 607, 780ff.; II, p. 373; Légasse, *Jésus et l'Enfant,* pp. 276ff.; cf. pp. 168ff.

43. cf. Jeremias, op. cit., pp. 48ff.; O. Cullmann, *Baptism in the*

New Testament, Studies in Biblical Theology, 1 (SCM Press, London, 1950), pp. 25f., 71ff.; Wohlenberg, op. cit., p. 272.

44. op. cit., pp. 48–55.

45. cf. M. Smith, op. cit., p. 169.

46. Cullmann, op. cit., pp. 71–80; and 'Les traces d'une vieille formule baptismale dans le Nouveau Testament', in *Revue d'Histoire et de Philosophie religieuses*, 17 (1937), pp. 424–34.

47. *Baptism in the New Testament* (Macmillan, London, 1962), pp. 320ff.; see also Légasse, *Jésus et l'Enfant*, pp. 210ff.; K. Aland, *Did the Early Church Baptize Infants?* (ET, SCM Press, London, 1963), pp. 95–9.

48. Dodd, op. cit., p. 359; cf. R. E. Brown, *The Gospel According to John*, vol. 1 (Doubleday, New York, 1966), pp. 141–4; R. Schnackenburg, *The Gospel According to St John*, vol. 1 (ET, Burns & Oates, London, and Herder & Herder, New York, 1968), pp. 366–8.

49. D. Daube, op. cit., p. 234; see all of pp. 224–46, and cf. our n. 37.

50. Luke uses it five times; it is not used by any of the other evangelists; cf. Légasse, *Jésus et l'Enfant*, p. 40; for the other Lucan modifications, see ibid., pp. 40f., 195–209.

51. cf. Légasse, *Jésus et l'Enfant*, p. 38.

52. op. cit., p. 190; cf. K. Weiss, 'Ekklesiologie, Tradition und Geschichte in der Jüngerunterweisung, Mark 8:27–10:52', in *Der historische Jesus und der kerygmatische Christus*, ed. H. Ristow and K. Matthiae (Berlin, 1961), pp. 414–38.

53. cf. Beasley-Murray, op. cit., p. 327.

54. cf. W. K. L. Clarke, *New Testament Problems* (SPCK, London, 1929), pp. 36–8; F. A. Schelling, 'What means the saying about receiving the kingdom of God as a little child?', in *Expository Times*, 77 (1965–66), pp. 56–8.

55. op. cit., p. 152.

56. ibid., p. 158.

57. ibid., p. 157.

58. And if Ambrozic is correct in tracing the earlier meanings given to the saying (op. cit., pp. 139ff.), then there is no violent change in the meaning of the saying in its present context.

59. op. cit., pp. 189ff.

60. This is the theme which Professor Barclay highlights in *Mark*

(Daily Study Bible, St Andrew Press, Edinburgh, 1954), p. 251.

61. This interpretation is not far removed from that of McDonald (art. cit.), who argues on the basis of Jewish parallels for the 'teachability and complete obedience of the child as he learns to receive the Kingdom'. 'Trust' and 'obedience' are linked terms. The slightly different emphasis we have given the concept arises, perhaps, from its present Hellenistically coloured atmosphere; McDonald was thinking of the original Jewish context of Jesus' words.

62. cf. Best, *The Temptation and the Passion*, Society for New Testament Studies, Monograph Series, 2 (Cambridge University Press, London, 1965), pp. 64–8, and references given there; see also now Ambrozic, op. cit., *passim*.

SOME GREEK WORDS WITH 'HEBREW' MEANINGS IN THE EPISTLES AND APOCALYPSE

1. *Die Offenbarung Jesu Christi: Johannes-Apokalypse*, Zürcher Bibelkommentare (Zürich, 1970), vol. III, chs 21, 23, appendix, lexicon, bibliography, pp. 339ff.

2. 916 different words (Brütsch, loc. cit.).

3. My own count is 110, of which 66 are LXX, i.e. 60%.

4. David Hill, *Greek Words and Hebrew Meanings*, Society for New Testament Studies, Monograph Series, 5 (Cambridge University Press, London, 1967).

5. Nigel Turner, 'Jewish and Christian Influence on New Testament Vocabulary', in *Novum Testamentum*, XVI, 2 (1974).

6. Recent studies in the grammar, syntax and language of the Apocalypse are M. Zerwick, *Biblical Greek* (Rome, 1963); C. G. Ozanne, 'The Language of the Apocalypse', in *The Tyndale House Bulletin*, 16 (April 1965), pp. 3–9 (also unpublished Ph.D. thesis, 'The Influence of the Text and Language of the Old Testament in the Book of Revelation' (1964)); G. Mussies, *The Morphology of Koine Greek as used in the Apocalypse of St John* (Leiden, 1971); A. Lancelloti, *Sintassi Ebraica nel Greco dell' Apocalisse* (Assisi, 1964).

7. So Ozanne, op. cit., p. 5.

8. International Critical Commentary, *Revelation*, vol. I (T. & T. Clark, Edinburgh, 1920), p. 170, ad 6:8.

9. See J. H. Moulton, G. Milligan, *Vocabulary of the Greek*

Testament (Hodder & Stoughton, London, 1930), s.v. θάνατος.

10. cf. H. G. Liddell, R. Scott, eds, *Greek-English Lexicon*, rev. ed. (Oxford University Press, Oxford, 1940), s.v. 'guide', 'govern'.

11. '... *weidende Tätigkeit vernichtende Folgen hat.* (*vgl. Jer. 22, 22 und s. E. Lohmeyer, Hdb, zu Apk 2, 27*).' So also Ozanne, op. cit., p. 5.

12. R. H. Charles, op. cit., pp. cxlviiff.

13. *The Original Language of the Apocalypse* (Toronto, 1928), p. 17.

14. op. cit., p. 14, ad 1:5.

15. The widely accepted conjecture of Professor David Daube that συγχρᾶσθαι at John 4:9 reflects a rabbinical prohibition of the use of the same (drinking) vessels by Jews and Samaritans, while scarcely a 'Semitism', falls, in my opinion, into the category of non-proven usages. Some of the main objections to Professor Daube's well-known translation, 'for Jews do not use vessels together with Samaritans' (adopted by C. K. Barrett and the NEB), have been well stated by D. R. Hall ('The Meaning of συγχρᾶσθαι in John 4:9', in *Expository Times*, LXXXIII, 2 (1971), pp. 56ff.). While the Rabbinic ruling is not in question, the grammar is (there are no parallels to the dependence of the dative Σαμαρείταις on συν in the verb, and συγχρᾶσθαι belongs to a familiar group of compounds with συν with an object in the dative). While συγχρᾶσθαι is difficult to attest in the sense of 'have dealings with', χρᾶσθαι is regularly so used. Even more important is the objection (not raised by Hall) that there is no rabbinical (Hebrew or Aramaic) expression behind and corresponding to the alleged usage.

16. cf. Moulton-Milligan, op. cit., s.v.; and the detailed studies in J. B. Lightfoot, *Colossians and Philemon* (Macmillan, London, 1897), pp. 187ff.; and T. K. Abbott, *A Critical and Exegetical Commentary on the Epistles to the Ephesians and to the Colossians* (T. & T. Clark, Edinburgh, 1897), pp. 257ff.

17. The force of the ἐκ in ἀπεκδυσάμενοι; cf. Lightfoot, loc. cit.

18. cf. F. W. Blass, H. Debrunner, *A Greek Grammar of the New Testament*, trans. R. W. Funk (Cambridge University Press, London, 1961), § 316 (1); and Bauer, *Greek-English Lexikon*

of the New Testament, trans. W. Arndt and F. W. Gingrich (Cambridge University Press, London, 1957), s.v.

19. So Abbott, loc. cit.

20. loc cit.

21. *Theologisches Wörterbuch zum Neuen Testament,* II, p. 319, s.v. δύω.

22. Meyer, *Kommentar zum Neuen Testament* (Göttingen, 1964), ad. loc., p. 119, n. 2.'Ein Bild vom Kampf ἀπεκδ="entwaffnen" ist hier nicht notwendig angezeigt; *dazu fehlen auch alle Belege'* (my italics).

23. e.g. 1 Sam. 31:9.

24. LXX here reads κατέπιεν ὁ θάνατος ἰσχύσας, an unusual rendering of *laneṣaḥ:* for [*l*]*aneṣaḥ*=εἰς ν(ε)ῖκος, cf. Amos 1:11; 8:7; Job 36:7.

25. Revelation shares with 1 John the use of νικᾶν to describe the 'victory' of the Christian (e.g. 1 John 5:4, 5). In 1 John it is usually a victory over the world; in Revelation the verb is most frequently used absolutely, 'he that conquers, is victorious'.

26. cf. Charles, op. cit.

27. op. cit., p. 20.

28. *The Apocalypse of John* (Yale University Press, New Haven, 1958), p. 107.

29. Torrey, op. cit., would take 15:2 in the same way and render 'those who are innocent of the beast . . .', although his translation (p. 183) retains the familiar meaning. The main difficulty is the ἐκ. Ozanne (op. cit., p. 6) holds that the construction can be explained satisfactorily from Hebrew usage with the verb *ḥazaḳ,* which is followed by *min* (=ἐκ) when it means 'to prevail over', e.g. 1 Sam. 17:50: 'So David prevailed over the Philistine . . .' This Hebrew verb, however, is never rendered by νικᾶν in the LXX. Could this be the *min*=ἐκ of comparison or superiority over?

30. In the case of Lucan usage, Syriac influence seems more likely than the influence of Palestinian Aramaic.

31. See my *An Aramaic Approach to the Gospels and Acts,* 3rd ed. (Oxford University Press, London, 1967), pp. 108–12; and Blass-Debrunner, *A Greek Grammar of the New Testament,* § 258 (2).

32. Delling, in *Theologisches Wörterbuch zum Neuen Testament,* is an exception. See below.

33. cf. C. C. Torrey, op. cit., p. 113: 'The Aramaic word for "hour" is commonly used for the briefest space of time, English "moment". A good example is Dan. 4:16 (Engl. 4: 19).' Torrey seeks to apply this use to Rev. 8:1: '. . . there was silence in heaven for about half a minute.' It seems to me to be more than doubtful, however, if 8:1 can be so explained. It seems more likely that the expression here means 'half a year', and that the reference is to Dan. 7:25, which is interpreted at Rev. 12:14 as meaning 42 months, i.e. 3 years and half a year. (The sense 'year' for ὥρα is well-attested: see Liddell and Scott, s.v.) This is how the Syriac version in Land's *Anecdota Syriaca* (ii 61. 22, 73. 2) understands ἡμίσυ καιροῦ (*pelguṭ ša'ta*, i.e., lit. 'half an hour'), exactly as at Rev. 8:1.

34. *Theologisches Wörterbuch zum Neuen Testament*, IX, p. 681, n. 41, s.v. ὥρα.

35. The text at 18:10 is μιᾷ ὥρᾳ, but Westcott-Hort give μίαν ὥραν in the margin. The latter is probably a correction to the more regular accusative of duration of time as at Dan. 4:16, LXX, Theod.

36. cf. Delling, loc. cit.

37. cf. N. Turner, *A Grammar of New Testament Greek*, vol. III (T. & T. Clark, Edinburgh, 1906), p. 57, where ἀδικεῖσθε here is rendered by 'submit to fraud'.

38. cf. Blass-Debrunner, *A Grammar of the New Testament*, § 351 (2).

39. In *Theologisches Wörterbuch zum Neuen Testament*, I, p. 157, s.v. ἀδικεῖν.

40. These two passages remind one of E. Käsemann's 'Sätze heiligen Rechtes im Neuen Testament'. See the article with this title in *New Testament Studies*, I (1954–55), pp. 248–60; cf. also K. Berger, 'Zu den sogenannten Sätze heiligen Rechtes', in *New Testament Studies*, XVII (1970–71), pp. 10–40.

41. Charles, op. cit., vol. I, p. 59, ad 2:11; vol. II, p. 222, ad 22:11.

42. H. B. Swete, *The Apocalypse of St John* (Macmillan, London, 1907), ad loc.

43. ibid.

44. See my *Aramaic Approach to the Gospels and Acts*, p. 132.

45. cf. the extraordinary conjecture of Torrey, op. cit., pp. 99ff.

46. cf. Scott, op. cit., p. 19.
47. *Revelation*, vol. II, p. 199.
48. cf. ibid., vol. I, pp. 278, 286.
49. cf. Scott, op. cit., p. 13.
50. cf. Charles, op. cit., vol. I, p. 280.
51. cf. Charles, ad loc.
52. cf. Ozanne, op. cit., p. 8. It is unnecessary to presuppose that the dative reflects a *lāmeḏ* of definition: ταῖς χρειαῖς seems a regular Hellenistic Greek dative of respect.

APOLLOS THE ALEXANDRIAN

1. *The History of Primitive Christianity*, vol. I (Macmillan, London, 1937), p. 317.
2. P. T. Forsyth, *The Justification of God* (Latimer House, London, 1948), p. 218.
3. *Studies in the Gospels and Epistles* (Manchester University Press, Manchester, 1962), p. 257.
4. John Duncan, *Colloquia Peripatetica*, 6th ed. (Oliphant, Edinburgh and London, 1907), p. 59.

GLORY TO GOD IN THE HIGHEST. AND ON EARTH?

1. See A. Merx, *Die vier kanonischen Evangelien nach ihrem ältesten bekannten Texte*, II, 2: *Markus und Lukas* (Berlin, 1905), p. 200.
2. Harnack, in *Studien*, I (Berlin, 1931), pp. 158ff., argues for a different division of the words (and note he would omit ἐν before ἀνθρώποις):
   1st colon: δόξα ἐν ὑψίστοις θεῷ καὶ ἐπὶ γῆς
   2nd colon: εἰρήνη ἀνθρώποις εὐδοκίας.
   In favour of this division is the fact that the Greek syllables are more even (12, 10 against 8, 14) and that ἐπὶ γῆς might be thought superfluous with ἀνθρώποις. Against Harnack's division, I should argue that the parallelism of ideas is destroyed. (His attempt to meet this, which he admits is the strongest objection, is found on p. 162.) In place of 'heaven' and 'earth', Harnack offers 'heaven and earth' in the first line, and 'men' in the second.
3. C. H. Hunzinger, *Zeitschrift für die neutestamentliche Wissenschaft*, 44 (1952–53), pp. 85–90; *ZNW*, 49 (1958), pp. 129f.; J. A. Fitzmyer, in *Theological Studies*, 19 (1958), pp. 225–7,

reprinted in *Essays on the Semitic Background of the New Testament* (Geoffrey Chapman, London, 1971); R. Deichgräber, *ZNW*, 51 (1960), p. 132.

4. *Otium Norvicense, Pars Tertia: Notes on Select Passages of the Greek Testament Chiefly with Reference to Recent English Versions* (Oxford, 1881), p. 37 and n. 1. He cites 2 Sam. 16:7; 18:20; Pss. 80:18; 119:24; Jer. 15:10; Dan. 10:11; Obad. 7, in various versions.

NEW TESTAMENT CHRISTOLOGY IN A PLURALISTIC AGE

1. Oxford University Press, London, 1967, pp. 310–28.
2. *Encyclopedia Biblica*, vol. II, col. 1881.
3. SCM Press, London, 1950.

CAMBRIDGE SYRIAC FRAGMENT XXVI

1. C. J. Clay, London, 1900, pp. 94–7.
2. ibid., p. vii.
3. ibid., p. xviii.
4. 18 August 1900, col. 2209.
5. *Apocrypha Syriaca*, Studia Syriaca, xi (Cambridge, 1902), introduction, p. xxix.
6. *Palestinian Syriac Texts*, p. xx.
7. Nestorian MSS.: B.M. Add. 14440 (10th/11th cent.); Cambridge Add. 1964 (13th cent.); Mingana 504 (14th cent.); B.M.Add. 12138 ('punctuation' MS.; 9th cent.).
8. Jacobite MSS.: Bodleian Poc. 391 (17th cent.); Bodleian Or. 141 (17th cent.); B. M. Egerton 704 (17th cent.). The Buchanan Bible, Cambridge Oo. 1.1.2, is a Jacobite MS. of the 12th cent. It supports those three late Jacobite texts in the first and third entries in the table, but in the second entry it agrees with Walton and the Nestorian MSS. On the evidence of the manuscripts examined it may be said that the Buchanan Bible contains an early Jacobite element in its text and this always has the support of the three late Jacobite MSS., but on the other hand those three MSS. also contain early Jacobite readings that are not in the Buchanan Bible.

Books by William Barclay

1951   *Ambassador for Christ*, Church of Scotland Youth Committee, Edinburgh

1952   *And Jesus Said*, Church of Scotland Youth Committee, Edinburgh

1953–
1959   *The Daily Study Bible*, St Andrew Press, Edinburgh: *Acts* (1953); *Luke* (1953); *Corinthians* (1954); *Galatians and Ephesians* (1954); *Mark* (1954); *Hebrews* (1955); *John*, vols. 1 and 2 (1955); *Romans* (1955); *Matthew*, vol. 1 (1956); *Timothy, Titus, Philemon* (1956); *Matthew*, vol. 2 (1957); *John and Jude* (1958); *James and Peter* (1958); *Philippians, Colossians, Thessalonians* (1959); *Revelation*, vols. 1 and 2 (1959)

1955   *And He Had Compassion on Them*, St Andrew Press, Edinburgh

      A New Testament Wordbook, SCM Press, London

1957   *Letters to the Seven Churches*, SCM Press, London

1957–   *Daily Bible Readings* (with commentary by Barclay), Committee on Publications, Church of Scotland, Edinburgh

1958   *The Mind of St Paul*, Collins, London

      More New Testament Words, SCM Press, London

1959   *Educational Ideals in the Ancient World*, Collins, London

      The Master's Men, SCM Press, London

      The Plain Man's Book of Prayers, Fontana Books, London

      The Way, the Truth and the Life (Ralph P. Coleman's paintings, with accompanying text by Barclay), Collins, London

1960   *The Mind of Jesus*, SCM Press, London

      The Promise of the Spirit, Epworth Press, London

1961   *Crucified and Crowned*, SCM Press, London

      The Making of the Bible, Lutterworth, London, and Abingdon Press, New York and Nashville

1961–   *Bible Guides* (edited jointly with F. F. Bruce), Lutterworth, London, and Abingdon Press, New York and Nashville

1962   *The Christian Way*, St Andrew Press, Edinburgh: I. *The Christian Way*; II. *Talking and Listening to God*; III. *The Christian Guide Book*; IV. *The Church and You*; V. *You and the Church*; VI. *The Sacred Service of the Church*
Flesh and Spirit (an examination of Galatians 5:19–23), SCM Press, London
Jesus as They Saw Him, SCM Press, London
More Prayers for the Plain Man, Fontana Books, London

1963   *Christian Discipline in Society Today* (Alex Wood Memorial Lecture), Fellowship of Reconciliation, New Malden
Epilogues and Prayers, SCM Press, London
Many Witnesses, One Lord, SCM Press, London
The Plain Man Looks at the Beatitudes, Fontana Books, London
Prayers for Young People, Fontana Books, London
Turning to God (A. S. Peake Memorial Lecture), Epworth Press, London

1964   *The All-Sufficient Christ* (Colossians), SCM Press, London
New Testament Words, SCM Press, London
The Plain Man Looks at the Lord's Prayer, Fontana Books, London
Prayers for the Christian Year, SCM Press, London

1965   *Epistle to the Hebrews* (*Bible Guide*), Lutterworth Press, London
A New People's Life of Jesus, SCM Press, London
The New Testament in Historical and Contemporary Perspective (edited jointly with H. Anderson), Blackwell, Oxford

1966   *The First Three Gospels*, SCM Press, London
Fishers of Men, Epworth Press, London
Seen in the Passing (edited by Rita F. Snowden), Collins, London

1967   *The Lord's Supper*, SCM Press, London
The Plain Man Looks at the Apostles' Creed, Fontana Books, London
Thou Shalt Not Kill, Fellowship of Reconciliation, New Malden

1968   *The Bible and History* (editor), Lutterworth Press, London
Communicating the Gospel, Drummond Press, Stirling
The New Testament, vol. I, *Gospels and Acts of the Apostles* (Professor Barclay's own translation), Collins, London
Prayers for Help and Healing, Fontana Books, London

1969   *The King and the Kingdom*, St Andrew Press, Edinburgh
The New Testament, vol. II, *The Letters and the Revelation* (Professor Barclay's own translation), Collins, London

1970   *God's Young Church*, St Andrew Press, Edinburgh

1971 *Camp Prayers and Services*, Boys' Brigade, London
Ethics in a Permissive Society, Collins and Fontana Books, London
Through the Year with William Barclay (edited by Denis Duncan), Hodder & Stoughton, London

1972 *Introducing the Bible*, Bible Reading Fellowship, London, and Denholm House Press, Redhill
The Old Law and the New Law, St Andrew Press, Edinburgh

1973 *By What Authority?*, Darton, Longman & Todd, London
Every Day with William Barclay (edited by Denis Duncan), Hodder & Stoughton, London
Marching Orders (edited by Denis Duncan), St Andrew Press, Edinburgh, and Hodder & Stoughton, London
The Plain Man's Guide to Ethics, Fontana Books, London

1974 *Jesus Christ for Today*, Methodist Church Division of Home Mission, London
Marching On, St Andrew Press, Edinburgh, and Hodder & Stoughton, London

1975 *Testament of Faith*, Mowbray, Oxford
undated *The Christian and his Prayers*, St Andrew Press, Edinburgh